STEVEN SPIELBERG

Recent Titles in Greenwood Biographies

STEVEN SPIELBERG

A Biography

Kathi Jackson

GREENWOOD BIOGRAPHIES

GREENWOOD PRESS
WESTPORT, CONNECTICUT . LONDON

Library of Congress Cataloging-in-Publication Data

Jackson, Kathi, 1951–
   Steven Spielberg : a biography / Kathi Jackson.
      p. cm. — (Greenwood biographies ISSN 1540–4900)
   Includes bibliographical references and index.
   ISBN-13: 978–0–313–33796–3 (alk. paper)
   ISBN-10: 0–313–33796–9 (alk. paper)
 1. Spielberg, Steven, 1946– 2. Motion picture producers and
directors—United States—Biography. I. Title.
   PN1998.3.S65J33 2007
   791.43023'3092—dc22
   [B]   2006039109

British Library Cataloguing in Publication Data is available.

Library of Congress Catalog Card Number: 2006039109

ISBN-13: 978–0–313–33796–3
ISBN-10: 0–313–33796–9
ISSN: 1540–4900

First published in 2007

Greenwood Press, 88 Post Road West, Westport, CT 06881
An imprint of Greenwood Publishing Group, Inc.
www.greenwood.com

Printed in the United States of America

The paper used in this book complies with the
Permanent Paper Standard issued by the National
Information Standards Organization (Z39.48–1984).

10 9 8 7 6 5 4 3 2 1

Copyright Acknowledgments

The author and publisher gratefully acknowledge permission for use of the following
material:

Richard Combs, "Primal Scream: An Interview with Steven Spielberg." First published
in *Sight and Sound*, Spring 1977. Reprinted in *Steven Spielberg Interviews*, edited by Lester
D. Friedman and Brent Notbohm (Jackson: University of Mississippi, 2000). Permission
granted by Richard Combs, July 16, 2006.

Frank Sanello, *Spielberg: The Man, The Movies, The Mythology* (Dallas: Taylor
Publishing, 1996). Permission granted by Patricia Zline, Rowman Littlefield Publishing
Group. Lanham, MD.

Lester D. Friedman and Brent Notbohm, eds. *Steven Spielberg Interviews* (Jackson:
University of Mississippi, 2000).

Every reasonable effort has been made to trace the owners of copyright materials in this
book, but in some instances this has proven impossible. The author and publisher will be
glad to receive information leading to more complete acknowledgments in subsequent
printings of the book and in the meantime extend their apologies for any omissions.

CONTENTS

Photo essay follows page 64

SERIES FOREWORD

In response to high school and public library needs, Greenwood developed this distinguished series of full-length biographies specifically for student use. Prepared by field experts and professionals, these engaging biographies are tailored for high school students who need challenging yet accessible biographies. Ideal for secondary school assignments, the length, format, and subject areas are designed to meet educators' requirements and students' interests.

Greenwood offers an extensive selection of biographies spanning all curriculum related subject areas including social studies, the sciences, literature and the arts, history and politics, as well as popular culture, covering public figures and famous personalities from all time periods and backgrounds, both historic and contemporary, who have made an impact on American and/or world culture. Greenwood biographies were chosen based on comprehensive feedback from librarians and educators. Consideration was given to both curriculum relevance and inherent interest. The result is an intriguing mix of the well known and the unexpected, the saints and sinners from long-ago history and contemporary pop culture. Readers will find a wide array of subject choices from fascinating crime figures like Al Capone to inspiring pioneers like Margaret Mead, from the greatest minds of our time like Stephen Hawking to the most amazing success stories of our day like J. K. Rowling.

While the emphasis is on fact, not glorification, the books are meant to be fun to read. Each volume provides in-depth information about the subject's life from birth through childhood, the teen years, and adulthood. A thorough account relates family background and education, traces

personal and professional influences, and explores struggles, accomplish-
ments, and contributions. A timeline highlights the most significant life
events against a historical perspective. Bibliographies supplement the reference value of each volume.

ACKNOWLEDGMENTS

Thanks to Heather Staines for welcoming me to Greenwood. Thanks to Kristi Ward for being so much fun to work with.

To my longtime friend Cheryl Smith, for answering questions that erased my worries.

To my teacher, mentor, and friend Birdie Etchison, for always being there with reassurance.

To Steven Awalt, editor at SpielbergFilms.com, for clarifying so many things. Steven, I can't thank you enough for all of your help. If I've not met your expectations, I'm really sorry. I tried.

Thank you, Aura Levin Lipski, publisher of www.Hebrewsongs.com, for verifying the name of the children's song in *Schindler's List*.

Thanks to all my friends and family for continued support, and most of all, thanks to my always loving best friend and husband, William.

INTRODUCTION:
THE SPIELBERG MYSTIQUE

Unlike actors and singers, there are just a handful of movie directors who are known worldwide and whose very name means success. Add the word "magic" and you have narrowed the list down to two: Walt Disney and Steven Spielberg. The two share another commonality: many of their films leave warm memories with their audiences. Spielberg knew from a very early age that he wanted to make movies. When Arnold Spielberg told his young son that he would have to start at the bottom of the movie business and work his way up, young Steven responded, "No, Dad. The first picture I do, I'm going to be a director."[1] He is said to have told a classmate, "I want to be the Cecil B. DeMille of science fiction."[2]

Spielberg fills 12 pages on the Internet's International Movie Database, and he has credits in each of the site's 11 categories: producer, director, miscellaneous crew, writer, editor, actor, second unit director or assistant director, visual effects, self (documentaries), archive footage, and notable TV guest appearances. He has won two Academy Awards for Best Director and the Academy's Irving Thalberg Lifetime Achievement Award. According to Yahoo! Spielberg "has succeeded in combining the intimacy of a personal vision with the epic requirements of the modern commercial blockbuster."[3] And most importantly, he "possesses an uncanny knack for eliciting and manipulating audience response."[4] And though money was never the object of his filmmaking, he is the most financially successful filmmaker in motion picture history and has been on *Forbes* annual list of richest people since at least 1997.

But except for making him more philanthropic, success has not changed this world-renowned giant of movies. He still wears jeans, sneakers, and a baseball cap. He still wears a beard and he still wears glasses. He does not drink, take drugs, or smoke. His only vice is biting his nails, which he has done since he was four years old. And although he turned 60 in 2006, he still has the abundance of fears and phobias that he has had all of his life. He has nightmares about floods, sharks, heights, and elevators. He is even scared of furniture with feet or decorations of snakes and insects. (Trivia: These phobias have not stopped him, however, from owning a house on the beach and a home in Trump Tower.) He has been happily married to the same woman, actress Kate Capshaw, since October 12, 1991, and has always put his family ahead of his career. He drives his children to school and often takes the family with him on location. And while he and his filmmaker friends may talk about business and make million-dollar deals, they are just as likely to talk about their kids' soccer games while their wives are doing the same in another room. According to his March 21, 1999, article in *The Guardian Limited*, Stephen J. Dubner writes that Spielberg's, "reach is so great and his power so boundless that, when people in Hollywood talk about him, it sounds as if they are talking about God, with one difference: people are not afraid to bad-mouth God."[5] Actor Tom Cruise says that Spielberg has not lost the decency that many others lose. "Even his detractors," writes Dubner, "who assault his films off the record, acknowledge that Spielberg is a ferocious multi-tasker, an idea machine and a canny businessman who has also managed to become a devout family man."[6] He is so good at what he does that his movies have become part of the American lexicon. "He is arguably the most influential popular artist of the 20th Century,"[7] says author Michael Crichton.

To Steven Spielberg, making movies is therapy, and he will readily tell you that he uses aspects of his childhood in almost every film: shooting stars, broken family, lonely child, piano, fatherless home, and the suburban neighborhood. Another of his trademarks is to use the "everyman" as his main character. This is the ordinary person who learns that he can accomplish far more than he thought he could—a character who creates a bond with the average moviegoer. All of these contribute to Spielberg's belief that his films are successful because they reach people on a human level. "You have to like the people of your story; it's very important, and if you don't like the people, no matter how technologically superior a film is, it's just not going to succeed."[8] An example of this technique is also one of his favorite scenes in *Jaws*. A depressed Police Chief Brody is oblivious to his little boy imitating his every gesture and expression. When Brody sees what is going on, he and the boy share a "soft moment. It's little things like that," says

Spielberg, "that I'm able to interject in terms of humanizing my movies."[9] "Each of my movies has showed enough humanity to allow the
audience to identify with the person who is having the experience."[10]

But Spielberg can also frighten the audience, and he uses suspense
and editing techniques like Alfred Hitchcock did. He also admires John
Ford's "judicious"[11] use of close-ups and wide shots and says that there
is, "nothing worse than a close-up that's from the chin to the forehead.
I remember watching *Paths of Glory* and realizing how few tight close-
ups there were, but when [Stanley] Kubrick used a close-up, it meant
something."[12] In *Badlands* and *Barry Lyndon,* says Spielberg, Kubrick
made you feel as if you were there. And John Frankenheimer's editing,
he says, "often has more energy than the content of the story. . . . When
I saw *The Manchurian Candidate*, I realized for the first time what film editing was all about."[13] When all is said and done, it is Stanley Kubrick's
Dr. Strangelove or How I Stopped Worrying and Learned to Love the Bomb
that Spielberg believes is "nearly a perfect motion picture." Its "broad,
baroque comedy," he says, "was extra funny"[14] because it was grounded
in reality.

Through the years as he learned more aspects of filmmaking, he says
that he wanted to do it all: gaffer, key grip, set design, makeup, composer,
etc. But he also learned that once you are on a professional filming site,
you fall under the rules of unions and are not allowed to do anyone else's
job. "Now," he says, "I delegate happily the functions that I feel there are
people much better equipped to execute than I am."[15] But he continues to
give his input regarding these aspects because he feels that it is his responsibility to the story. He still sets up the cameras and, although he is willing
to listen to editors, he still believes that "editing is my thing, as well as
cinematography."[16] When it comes to casting, Spielberg considers it "at
least half the movie . . . not only casting the actor, but also casting the
crew."[17] Once casting is completed, he feels that 40 percent of his creative
effort has been realized. He tries to hire actors who are not yet well known
so the audience cannot relate to his or her former roles and because new-
comers give so much, "all that energy and ambition."[18] He tries to turn
co-workers into a "family" and tries to bring out the best in his actors,
but he admits that he can be demanding and can forget the actors' needs.
"I see only the work, and sometimes I forget that there are a lot of human
people who are trying to contribute to your vision."[19] He adds, "Movies
are my sin; my major sin is filmmaking. I find the people who drink exces-
sively, or take a lot of drugs, aren't very happy with their lives and what
they're doing. But I've always been very happy making films and that is all
the stimulation that I've needed."[20]

He is always open to any ideas to improve his work, even if it means *not* using painstakingly made plans, and he always listens to suggestions from those around him. He knows better than to give in to either his controlling side or his creative side because each side must be represented. He is also known for the speed at which he films. He likes to get everyone going and then keep the momentum. One of his filming techniques is to keep cameras rolling—no constant retakes and cuts—and have the actors keep repeating the scene until everyone is satisfied, and he always prints his first takes because he often likes the actors' mistakes. Likewise, after a scene has been filmed several times, he will often throw in something to disconcert the actors. "Then I watch them scrambling for their confidence and scurrying for the focus of the scene. During that searching, some very exciting things can happen in front of the camera."[21] After he finishes a film, he feels that it is no longer his. He also fears that he would want to change too much of it. Besides, by that time he is ready to move on to another project. "I marvel at [composer] John Williams," he says, "because he can conduct his own music over and over again. I can't do that. I'll dedicate two—three years of my life to one film. But then I want to move on and try something new."[22]

Spielberg makes movies because he loves to make them, but his favorite part of the process is solitary—the excitement of getting a new idea and researching it and then deciding how to make it come to life on the screen. He also enjoys collaborating during which he says he gets his best ideas. No matter how he makes his movies, the results are loved because he follows his heart and does what he loves, even when some people say that his films are too sappy and predictable. He wants people to like his movies, and he is proud that entire families can watch them. "I always like to think of the audience when I am directing," he says, "Because I am the audience."[23] And as the audience, what are Spielberg's favorite movies? The list of ten is: *Fantasia* (1940), *Citizen Kane* (1941), *A Guy Named Joe* (1943), *It's a Wonderful Life* (1946), *The War of the Worlds* (1953), *Psycho* (1960), *Lawrence of Arabia* (1962), *2001: A Space Odyssey* (1968), *The Godfather* (1972) and *La Nuit américaine* (1973).

NOTES

1. Quoted in Joseph McBride, *Steven Spielberg: A Biography* (New York: Simon & Schuster, 1997), 13.

2. Ibid.

3. Yahoo! Movies, "Steven Spielberg Biography," www.movies.yahoo.com. (accessed April 18, 2006).

4. Ibid.

5. Stephen J. Dubner, "Steven the Good," *The New York Times Magazine*, February 14, 1999. Reprinted in *Steven Spielberg Interviews*, Lester D. Friedman and Brent Notbohm, eds. (Jackson: University Press of Mississippi, 2000), 225.

6. Ibid.

7. Quoted in McBride, 9.

8. Quoted in Susan Royal, "Always: An Interview with Steven Spielberg," *American Premiere*, December/January 1989–1990. Reprinted in *Steven Spielberg Interviews*, Lester D. Friedman and Brent Notbohm, eds. (Jackson: University Press of Mississippi, 2000), 90.

9. Quoted in Mitch Tuchman, "Close Encounter with Steven Spielberg," *Film Comment*, January/February 1978. Reprinted in *Steven Spielberg Interviews*, Lester D. Friedman and Brent Notbohm, eds. (Jackson: University Press of Mississippi, 2000), 44.

10. Quoted in Tuchman, 43.

11. Quoted in David Helpern, "At Sea with Steven Spielberg," *Take One*, March/April 1974. Reprinted in *Steven Spielberg Interviews*, Lester D. Friedman and Brent Notbohm, eds. (Jackson: University Press of Mississippi, 2000), 13.

12. Quoted in Richard Combs, "Primal Scream," *Sight & Sound*, Spring 1977. Reprinted in *Steven Spielberg Interviews*, Lester D. Friedman and Brent Notbohm, eds. (Jackson: University Press of Mississippi, 2000), 36.

13. Quoted in Combs, 35–36.

14. Quoted in Chris Hodenfield, "1941: Bombs Away," *Rolling Stone*, January 24, 1980. Reprinted in *Steven Spielberg Interviews*, Lester D. Friedman and Brent Notbohm, eds. (Jackson: University Press of Mississippi, 2000), 81.

15. Quoted in Steve Poster, "The Mind Behind *Close Encounters of the Third Kind*," *American Cinematographer*, February 1978. Reprinted in *Steven Spielberg Interviews*, Lester D. Friedman and Brent Notbohm, eds. (Jackson: University Press of Mississippi, 2000), 61.

16. Quoted in Poster, 62.

17. Quoted in Royal, 92.

18. Ibid.

19. Quoted in Royal, 93.

20. Quoted in Royal, 103.

21. Quoted in Royal, 91.

22. Quoted in Royal, 98.

23. Quoted in International Movie Database, "Biography for Steven Spielberg," www.imdb.com. (accessed September 22, 2005).

TIMELINE: SIGNIFICANT EVENTS IN THE LIFE OF STEVEN SPIELBERG

The years listed for the movies are the years they were released. Most were made the previous year.

February 25, 1945	Arnold Spielberg weds Leah Posner.
December 18, 1946	Steven Allan Spielberg is born in Cincinnati, Ohio.
1946–49	The family lives in a Jewish neighborhood, Avondale. In 1949, the family moves to New Jersey. Anne Spielberg is born December 25, 1949.
1952	Steven sees his first movie, *The Greatest Show on Earth*.
1953	Susan Spielberg is born December 4.
1956	Nancy Spielberg is born June 7.
1957	The Spielbergs move to Phoenix, the place Steven considers his true boyhood home.
1958	Steven falls in love with television and old movies and makes his first film, *The Last Train Wreck*.
1958–1959	Steven joins the Flaming Arrow Patrol of Ingleside's (Boy Scout) Troop 294, and makes *The Last Gun* to earn a Boy Scout badge.
1960	Makes *Fighter Squad*.
1962	Makes *Escape to Nowhere*, his first fully scripted movie, and wins First Prize at the Arizona Amateur Film Festival.

March 24, 1964	His first feature-length movie, *Firelight*, is shown at the Phoenix Little Theater.
March 25, 1964	The Spielbergs move to California.
1964–1965	Spends summers with an uncle who lives near Los Angeles so he can work at Universal Studios.
1965	Graduates from Saratoga High School.
1966	Arnold and Leah Posner separate. Arnold moves to Los Angeles. Leah and children move back to Phoenix. Steven begins attending California State College at Long Beach. Arranges classes so he can spend three days per week at Universal Studios. Lives with father the first year.
1967	The Spielbergs' divorce becomes final and Leah marries Bernie Adler.
1968	Steven makes his calling card movie, *Amblin'*, and gets a seven-year contract with Universal. Quits school.
November 8, 1969	Makes his professional directing debut with an episode of *Night Gallery* on NBC.
1969–1973	Directs several television programs.
November 13, 1971	*Duel* is aired as the "ABC Movie of the Weekend." Receives critical acclaim.
1973	Writes story, *Ace Eli & Rodger of the Skies*, and receives his first theatrical credit.
April 5, 1974	His first feature movie, *The Sugarland Express*, opens to outstanding reviews. Besides directing, Spielberg shares story credit with Hal Barwood and Matthew Robbins.
1975	Directs his first hit, *Jaws*, which sets box-office records, turns summer into a blockbuster season, and sets the bar for future adventure movies.
1977	Writes and directs *Close Encounters of the Third Kind* and receives his first Academy Award nomination for Best Director.
1978	His first producing project, *I Wanna Hold Your Hand*.
1979	Directs *1941* and proves that even Spielberg can make mistakes. Leah and Bernie open a restaurant, The Milky Way, in Los Angeles, which has a kosher dairy-based menu.
1980	Produces *Used Cars*.

1981   Teams with George Lucas to begin the saga of Indiana Jones with *Raiders of the Lost Ark*. Spielberg receives his second Academy Award nomination for Best Director. Produces *Continental Divide*.

1982   Writes and produces *Poltergeist*. Directs and produces *E.T. the Extra-Terrestrial* and receives his third Academy Award nomination for Best Director.

1983   Produces *Twilight Zone The Movie* and directs one segment.

1984   Joins Kathleen Kennedy and Frank Marshall to form Amblin Entertainment. Directs *Indiana Jones and the Temple of Doom*. Meets future wife, Kate Capshaw, when she auditions for leading female role. Produces *Gremlins*.

1985   Directs *The Color Purple*. Becomes a father when girlfriend, Amy Irving, gives birth to Max on June 13, 1985. The couple marries on November 27, 1985. Produces *The Goonies, Back to the Future*, and *Young Sherlock Holmes*.

1986   Produces *The Money Pit* and *An American Tail*.

1985–1987   Produces the series and directs two episodes of *Amazing Stories* for NBC—an unsuccessful return to television.

1987   Directs and produces *Empire of the Sun*. Produces *Innerspace* and **batteries not included*.

1988   Produces *Who Framed Roger Rabbit* and *The Land Before Time*.

1989   Directs *Indiana Jones and the Last Crusade*. Directs and produces *Always*, an updated version of *A Guy Named Joe* (1943). Divorces Amy Irving. Receives the Boys Scouts' Distinguished Eagle Scout Award. Produces *Back to the Future II* and *Dad*.

1990   Renews his relationship with Kate Capshaw and they have a daughter, Sasha. Produces *Back to the Future III, Gremlins2, Arachnophobia, Joe Versus the Volcano*, and TV's "Tiny Toon Adventures."

1991   Spielberg and Capshaw marry October 12. He and Capshaw adopt a son, Theo. Directs *Hook*. Produces *An American Tail: Fievel Goes West*.

1992   He and Capshaw have a son, Sawyer.

1993   Directs *Jurassic Park*. Directs and produces *Schindler's List*. The movie gives Spielberg his first Best Director Oscar. It also wins the Oscar for Best Picture. Produces TV series "Animaniacs" and *We're Back! A Dinosaur's Story*.

1994   Establishes Survivors of the Shoah Visual History Foundation to save Holocaust survivors' stories. Joins Jeffrey Katzenberg and David Geffen to form DreamWorks SKG. Produces *The Flintstones* and the TV series "ER"

1995   Produces *Casper* and *Balto*. Bernie Adler dies.

1996   He and Capshaw have another daughter, Destry, and adopt a daughter, Mikaela. Produces *Twister*.

1997   Directs *The Lost World Jurassic Park*. Directs and produces *Amistad*. Produces *Men in Black*. Arnold Spielberg marries Bernice Colner.

1998   Directs and produces *Saving Private Ryan*. Wins second Best Director Oscar. Produces *Deep Impact* and *The Mask of Zorro*.

1999   Directs *American Journey* (aka *The Unfinished Journey*).

2000   DreamWorks Interactive Studio is sold to Electronic Arts.

2001   Writes, directs, and produces *A.I. Artificial Intelligence*. Produces *Jurassic Park III* and the TV mini-series, "Band of Brothers." Resigns from Boy Scouts' Advisory Board because of their view on homosexuality.

2002   Directs *Minority Report*. Directs and produces *Catch Me If You Can*. Produces *Men in Black II* and the TV mini-series, "Taken." Graduates from California State University at Long Beach.

2004   Directs and produces *The Terminal*.

2005   Directs *War of the Worlds*. Directs and produces *Munich*. Produces *The Legend of Zorro*, *Memoirs of a Geisha*, and the TV mini-series, "Into the West." Announces that he will help develop three games for Electronic Arts. Except for DreamWorks Animation SKG, Spielberg, Katzenberg, and Geffen sell DreamWorks SKG to Paramount Pictures for $1.6 million.

2006   With director Zhang Yimou, Spielberg signs on
        to codesign the opening and closing ceremonies
        of the 2008 Beijing Olympics. Announces that
        he and Mark Burnett will produce *On the Lot*,
        a reality television program. Produces *Monster
        House*, *Flags of Our Fathers*, *Spell Your Name*, and
        Letters from Iwo Jima. As a producer, he has these
        projects in various phases of production.
        Note: Release dates are prone to change.

> *On the Lot* TV series (2007)
> "Nine Lives" (mini) TV Series (2007)
> *Transformers* (2007)
> *Disturbia* (2007)
> *The Talisman* (2008)
> *Jurassic Park IV* (2008)
> *When Worlds Collide* (2008)
> *Team of Rivals* (aka the Lincoln biopic) (2008)
> *Interstellar* (2009)
> "The Pacific War" (mini) TV Series (2009)

> As a director, he has these movies in various
> stages of production:

> *Team of Rivals* (aka the Lincoln biopic)
> (2008)
> *Indiana Jones 4* (2008)
> *Interstellar* (2009)

Chapter 1

THE FORMATIVE YEARS, 1946–1968

Once you learn about the life of Steven Spielberg, you begin to see examples of its influence in many of his movies. While other people pay counselors to listen to their childhood recollections, Spielberg makes money telling the world about his.

Arnold Spielberg and Leah Posner Spielberg lived in Cincinnati, Ohio, when their first child, Steven Allan, was born on December 18, 1946. For the next three years they lived in the Jewish neighborhood of Avondale, where Steven spent a lot of time with his maternal grandparents, "Mama" and "Dadda" Posner. One day the little boy and his mother were at a store and he wanted a toy Greyhound bus and threw a tantrum when she refused to buy it. The family rabbi happened to observe the incident and called "Mama" Posner, who, in typical grandmotherly fashion, promptly went out and bought the toy for her grandson. As she watched him play with it, she noticed how he balanced the bus on the table's edge with two of the wheels hanging over the side. In later years, she realized that she had witnessed his first experimentation with special effects. "You mark my words," she once said. "The world will hear of him."[1] Besides spoiling her grandson, Jennie Posner taught English to Holocaust survivors to help them become U.S. citizens. She was also an in-demand public speaker whose speaking voice, says her daughter, was "like a singing voice."[2] Philip Posner immigrated to the United States from Russia. Officially, he was in the clothing business, but he preferred to spend time dancing, playing the guitar, and telling stories. (One of his brothers was a Yiddish Shakespearean actor, and another brother danced and sang in vaudeville before becoming a lion tamer in the circus.) Once, when money ran low, he sold some jewelry and then took the family on a vacation. Leah Posner carries loving memories of an "exciting" man who walked with her through a snowstorm and lifted his head to the heavens and said, "How wondrous are thy works." To Leah, this was more than a loving image. "This is who I am," she says. "This is who Steven is."[3] She studied to become a concert pianist and says that such an accomplishment gave her confidence, but she gave up the piano when she married Arnold Spielberg on February 25, 1945. Outgoing and full of spirit, Leah rarely said "no" to her children. Compared to her husband's more pragmatic nature, it is easy to see why Leah was Steven's favorite parent.

Arnold Spielberg had an inquisitive technical mind and a career that required much of his time. He also earned many promotions, which meant that the family had to move every few years. As a child, Steven could not know and appreciate that his father was in on the ground floor of the computer industry and that he would eventually hold 12 patents. All the boy saw was a distant father who disrupted his young life with constant moving. And while the boy was awed by his father's war service, it is unlikely that he truly realized just what the man had accomplished during those years. Arnold Spielberg enlisted in the U.S. Army Signal Corps in January 1942. When he found himself in India working with aircraft parts and other war materiel, he asked to be assigned to the 490th Bombardment Squadron. He was promoted to master sergeant and became "an expert signalman." Using bamboo poles, he designed "a high gain, bi-directional rhombic antenna" whose signal was "clear as 'Ma Bell.'" He also made changes to radio equipment that enabled his base to use their only generator. During one task he nearly electrocuted himself but went on to rewire a circuit so the same thing would not happen to anyone else. Last but not least, Master Sergeant Spielberg flew combat missions into Imphal to deliver food and ammunition to British and Indian troops and bring out the wounded. Although it took many years, his contributions to the war effort were finally acknowledged. In 1999, he received the meritorious service award from the Selective Service system. In April 2000, his son honored him by donating the money to build a theatre at America's National D-Day Memorial. On April 6, 2001, Arnold Spielberg was awarded the Bronze Star Medal. Quoting the government tribute, "He set up the communications system that serviced the control tower for planes practicing strafing and bombing missions on an island in the Indian Ocean. He also started to train as a radio gunner and learned all about the B-25s, the famous Mitchell bomber, communication equipment, inside and out."[4]

FIRST ENCOUNTERS

Steven's first memory is of attending a Jewish temple (in Avondale) in his stroller and being awed by the red light that glowed in the sanctuary where the replica of the Ark of the Covenant is kept. This may be where he began his fascination with what he calls "God Lights."[5] That this should be his first memory is almost a revelation about how important his religion would become to him, though not for many years. When Steven was about three, the family moved to New Jersey. One starry night his dad put him into the car and drove him to a hilltop. With blanket in hand, father and son walked to the top of a hill, spread out the blanket, and sat down. The father pointed to the sky and showed his sun the Perseid meteor shower. Thus began Steven Spielberg's love affair with the sky that he has shared with millions of moviegoers. At the time, however, Steven says that his awe of what he observed was flawed when his dad added the scientific terms because it took away some of the mystery. But that was then. Today he quickly credits his father with introducing him to the magic of the sky.

THE FRIGHTENED AND FRIGHTENING CHILD

In an effort to protect their children (by June 1956, Steven was joined by sisters Anne, Sue, and Nancy), the Spielbergs rarely permitted the kids to watch television or go to movies, so Steven was thrilled when he saw his first movie, *The Greatest Show on Earth*. But the little boy was disappointed that there was no real circus on stage and that the movie was about adults with the only real excitement coming toward the end—a train wreck. And while the Spielbergs assumed that Walt Disney movies were the best for their children, they had no idea how much *Bambi* and *Snow White and the Seven Dwarfs* would frighten their very impressionable son. Steven Spielberg admits that he was, and still is, afraid of many things. As a child, he was terrified of swaying tree branches outside his bedroom window, clouds, wind, the dark, and clowns—even the shadow puppets he made on the ceiling. But he enjoyed the stimulation of being scared and soon learned that the best way to overcome your own fears is to frighten others, which he mercilessly did to his sisters. As Anne got older, she teamed with her brother to scare Sue and Nancy. Their mother often tells of the time that Steven put the head of one of Nancy's dolls on a bed of lettuce and served it to the little girl. There were also times when he would stand outside the girls' bedroom window and howl, "I am the moon." According to their mother, her daughters are still frightened by the moon. "Steven wasn't exactly cuddly," his mother says. "What he was was scary. When Steven woke up from a nap, I shook." But she quickly adds that she and the kids "had a great time."[6] In later years, Steven would produce *Poltergeist* (see chapter 3), which he says is, "the darker side of my nature—it's me when I was scaring my younger sisters half to death when we were growing up—and *E.T.* is my optimism about the future and my optimism about what it was like to grow up in Arizona and New Jersey."[7]

TRUE BOYHOOD HOME

In 1957, Arnold Spielberg took a job with General Electric, and the Spielbergs moved to the place that Steven still considers his true boyhood home: Phoenix, Arizona. Here he had the suburban home and family that he tries to recreate in so many of his movies. Here he finally had a dog (Thunder), a pet lizard, and even parakeets that freely flew inside the house. He watched television as much as he could—an escape that became his education. He loved comedians Imogene Coca, Sid Caesar, and Soupy Sales, and the TV show *The Honeymooners*. Television introduced him to many black-and-white movies and so fascinated him that he even enjoyed listening to the hissing and watching the "snow" when the channels ended their daily programming. He especially enjoyed Spencer Tracy, and Tracy's *Captains Courageous* inspired aspects of Spielberg's *Empire of the Sun* just as Tracy's *Adam's Rib* inspired the male-female aspects of the Indiana Jones movies. He also admired Frank Capra's work, particularly *It's a Wonderful Life*, with its depiction of the all-American community. He especially appreciates the way Capra filmed crowd scenes.

THE BOY SCOUTS

Another of Steven's passions was the Boy Scouts. He desperately wanted to earn the 21 merit badges necessary to become an Eagle Scout, but he had few talents and no athletic ability. For example, at a summer camp he demonstrated the proper way to sharpen an ax and sliced open one of his fingers. He did, however, become his troop's first Eagle Scout, and in high school he became a member of the Boy Scout Honor Society, the Order of the Arrow. In 1989, he was awarded the Distinguished Eagle Scout Award from the National Council of the Boy Scouts of America at their national jamboree. Spielberg believes in the values that scouting teaches, and he sees earning badges as a way to learn how to set goals and achieve them, but he left his position on its advisory board in April 2001. According to an article by Margaret Downey in July 2001 on the "Scouting for All" Web site, Spielberg said, "'The last few years in scouting have deeply saddened me to see the Boy Scouts of America actively and publicly participating in discrimination. It's a real shame.' With that, Spielberg announced that he had decided to quit the advisory board of the Boy Scouts of America after having been a member for 10 years. He had also donated money to fund camps, helped write the guidelines for a cinematography merit badge, and was honored by the Scouts several years prior at the group's quadrennial jamboree. He was also featured prominently in promotional material for the group. All that has come to an end thanks to Spielberg's consideration of the ethics involved in supporting a group that practices discrimination. Spielberg said he will continue to encourage the group to 'end this intolerance and discrimination once and for all.'"[8]

DISCOVERING THE CAMERA

The Spielbergs enjoyed trips to the White Mountains. At one point, Leah Spielberg gave her husband an 8mm camera with which to film their trips, but his results bored young Steven, who complained until his father gave him the camera. The trips then became directed and choreographed mini-movies: when and how to pack and unpack, when and how to exit the car, anything to turn a mundane experience into something interesting. When Steven was 11, his father threatened to take away his train set because he kept wrecking the cars. The boy realized that to keep the trains *and* continue the train-wreck experience, he could film the wreck. He called this, his first movie, *The Last Train Wreck*.

The Boy Scouts offered only a photography badge, but Steven convinced his scoutmaster to let him make a movie instead. With the help of his family, he filmed *The Last Gun* (aka *The Last Gunfight*, aka *The Last Shootout*) at Scottsdale's Pinnacle Peak Patio restaurant, chosen because it had an old stagecoach. In this, his first movie with a plot, the stagecoach driver is killed by bandanna-wearing, cap-pistol-carrying desperados who also rob a passenger (sister Anne) of her jewelry box. The film premiered in 1959 in front of his fellow Boy Scouts, and Steven earned not only his merit badge but also the cheers from a real audience—something he took to immediately.

The usual Steven Spielberg productions starred family, friends, and pets. *A Day in the Life of Thunder* (aka *This Is a Dog's Life*), made in 1958, was about a very muddy cocker spaniel named Thunder being washed by the girls and was told from Thunder's point of view. By the time the boy had made several movies, he knew that filmmaking was his future. "I had learned that film was power."[9] In fact, the shy little boy with poor grades who saw himself as a geek with a big nose was so transformed each time he got behind a camera that he became not only outgoing but demanding.

Arnold and Leah Spielberg encouraged their children to pursue their interests, but they also taught them to help with the expenses. One way Steven earned money for film was by whitewashing the neighbors' citrus trees—sometimes 30 trees a day—for 75 cents a tree. The family also helped him by showing rented movies to the neighborhood kids on summer Sunday nights. Arnold brought home a projector from work and rented the movies. Steven printed tickets that the girls sold door-to-door during the week. Leah made popcorn and sold it in brown paper sacks. The girls sold candy. Arnold hooked up speakers, and Steven covered the projector with a box so that its noise would not distract the audience. The film's images were shown through a hole in the box and onto a hanging bed sheet. He showed the movies he made as "shorts." Since it was not legal for the family to profit from the venture, they used what they needed to buy more supplies and film and then donated the profits to the Perry Institute, a home for mentally handicapped children. Not only did the activity make the money young Steven needed to buy film, but the events were publicized in the local newspaper. His mother called him "Cecil B. DeSpielberg."[10]

Ready to learn more, Steven asked his father for more sophisticated equipment and received a movie camera with a three-turret lens (standard, wide-angle, and telephoto). One of the first movies he made with his new camera was *Fighter Squad* (1960), inspired by his love of World War II, which was inspired by his father's World War II experiences. The young Spielberg must have been born with the "It never hurts to ask" gene, because he was never shy about asking people to help him in his ventures—and people rarely turned him down. (Trivia: He once got a hospital to close off the wing that included its emergency room so that he could film there.) For *Fighter Squad*, he convinced the Phoenix airport to let him use a real B-51. He had a friend put on Arnold Spielberg's bomber jacket and goggles and then put the friend into the pilot seat of the plane. Steven took a close-up shot of the stick being pulled back then cut to footage of a plane going into a climb. He cut back to a close-up of the pilot "grinning sadistically,"[11] then to a close-up of the pilot's thumb hitting the button. The scene ended with footage of a plane with its guns ablaze.

Steven also filmed high school football games and a gag documentary about a school outing. Sister Anne says, "The moment he started a project, it was like the Pied Piper. Everybody in the neighborhood wanted to have something to do with it,"[12] and even his sisters, always first in line, had to compete for parts, the winner chosen according to Steven's mood. Even the kids who ignored Steven in school competed to be in his films.

The problem, he says, was that they enjoyed it at first, but then grew bored. During the school year, they could work only on weekends, and as the boys grew older, most of them preferred to spend time with girls and cars. When some did not return, Steven had to rewrite and reedit. "That was a major problem," he says. "It still is a major problem!"[13] And while he remembers being unpopular, Anne says that many girls thought he was cute "in a nerdy way."[14] Steven says about himself, "I was skinny and unpopular. I was the weird, skinny kid with acne. I hate to use the word wimp, but I wasn't in the inner loop. I never felt comfortable with myself, because I was never part of the majority."[15] After purposely losing a race to a mentally retarded boy, he was often called "Retard."[16] He refers to the incident as "the height of my wimpery" and says, "I'd never felt better and I'd never felt worse in my life."[17] Sometimes he compares his youth to an American sitcom, "The kind that ABC buys for a season before they drop it."[18] When he found the courage to take a girl to the drive-in (in the fifth grade with his father driving), the girl put her head on his shoulder, and his parents later lectured him about promiscuity. In a scene partially recreated in *E.T.*, Steven got sick while dissecting a frog in biology class. He left the room and stood in the hall with the other "weak-stomached students"[19] who, to his dismay, were all girls. Gawky kids often find that they can make people laugh. Since Steven was not into comedy, he used his movies instead. (Trivia: Spielberg says that actor Eddie Deezen looks like he, Spielberg, did in school.)

RELIGION

Spielberg once called his family "storefront kosher"[20] because they did not practice their faith on a strict or regular basis. They did light candles on the Sabbath, went to temple on Friday nights and High Holy days, and Steven was bar mitzvahed in an Orthodox synagogue. But for most of his formative years, Steven was the only Jew he knew outside of his family, and each time the family moved, he had to assimilate again. Even though it was his mother's idea to live in gentile neighborhoods, Steven resented his father for causing the moves. It was easy for his father, he says, "My father assimilated into the gentile world of computers, and that's a very Wasp world."[21] The young boy was so desperate to be like the gentile kids that he even duct-taped his nose down to flatten it, and every Christmas he begged his dad to hang Christmas lights so their house would not be the only one on the block without them. He was even ashamed of his beloved grandfather with his long white beard who prayed in the corner of their home wearing a long black coat and a black hat. And he certainly did not like it when his grandfather called him by his Hebrew name, *Schmuel*.[22] Steven had heard bits and pieces about relatives killed in Poland and the Ukraine but he was too young to appreciate such sacrifices.

WINNING

Using Camelback Mountain Desert in Phoenix as North Africa, Steven filmed his first fully scripted movie in 1962. *Escape to Nowhere* was a 40-minute film about German Field Marshall Erwin Rommel fighting the Americans. Both parents wore fatigues and took turns driving a Jeep. Neighbor boys played both Americans and Germans, and because there were so few German helmets, boys would put one on, run by the camera, and then hand their helmet to someone else. Arnold Spielberg provided fireworks and what appeared to be explosions. *Escape to Nowhere* won first prize in the Arizona Amateur Film Festival. The prizes were a 16mm movie camera and some books on making movies. Steven promptly donated the books to his high school's library and traded in the camera for an 8mm Bolex and sound system. He learned that he could send cut footage to Eastman Kodak where a magnetic strip was placed on the film so he could add sound. He also learned that he could shoot, rewind, and shoot again. Now he could make double exposures, make people disappear, and turn "beautiful young women . . . into ghoulish nightmares."[23] When he purchased a polarizer, he could fade in and fade out. He filmed master shots on one roll of film, close-ups on another, and action/trick shots on a third. He would break down the film and hang the separate shots on his homemade cutting rack and then tape onto each scene its description and location in the film. In an interview many years later, Spielberg said, "I remember doing things at 16 that I was later surprised to see being done in 35mm in the movie theater."[24] Where did he learn all of this? It just seemed natural, he says.

It was with this new camera that Steven began making *Firelight*, his first feature-length movie and the one some say showed his "true potential as a filmmaker."[25] Inspired by the meteor shower he had watched with his dad so many years before, Steven wrote about aliens abducting earthlings for an extraterrestrial zoo. As before, he filmed on weekends during the school year using family, friends, and local college students. Anne was the typist and script girl, and Nancy was the star of the movie, the person abducted and killed by aliens. Steven's father invested in the film, rigged the lights, and built the set and anything else his son needed. His mother's serving cart became the dolly on which Steven sat holding the camera while Anne pushed him to where he wanted to go. But the topper may have been the special effects: 30 cans of cherry pie filling cooked in a pressure cooker until the lid blew off—instant gore! He filmed toy trucks and paper-mache mountains so they looked life-sized, and he did all of his own editing and splicing. The problem came in the summer when Steven needed to dub in the sound and many of the kids were busy elsewhere. He had to persuade them to recite their lines while trying to match their words to their scenes in the movie. *Firelight* was complete with soundtrack and sound effects. (Steven is self-taught on clarinet and organ so he made his own score.) Arnold Spielberg rented the Phoenix Little Theater for the night of March 24, 1964. Leah put the letters on the marquee and sold tickets for one dollar. The movie cost $400 and brought in $600. (Sadly, little of *Firelight* remains today.)

CALIFORNIA

But the very next day, the Spielbergs moved once again, this time to Saratoga, California. Arnold Spielberg's talent had earned him yet another promotion, and they were now moving to the area that would soon be known as "Silicon Valley." Moving never got easier, says Steven.

A "C" student all through high school, the only reading that Steven enjoyed was film magazines, science-fiction stories, and *MAD* magazine. He was particularly bad in math and admits he still cannot perform fractions. Although his father helped with his movie making, he continued to hope that Steven would go to college and even got him up early every morning to help him with math—another reason that Steven resented his father. Father and son often argued and, as happens in so many families, they were estranged for a number of years and then became good friends. After this move, the young man ignored filmmaking to concentrate on his studies. "I was trying to get out of high school, get some decent grades, and find a college,"[26] he says. But life got harder for the young man, because it was in Saratoga that he experienced true anti-Semitism for the first time. In school, students hit him, threw pennies at him, and called him "Jew." Once someone threw a cherry bomb between his legs while he sat on the toilet. Another time someone ground his face in the dirt. Being treated differently because of his religion scared and angered him. After he had twice come home with a bloody nose, his mother began picking him up after school. "To this day," says Spielberg, "I haven't gotten over it, nor have I forgiven any of them."[27] (Nor will he put up with anti-Semitism. At a car dealership, he placed an order for a car, drove away, and then learned that his salesman said, "I just got a Jew to pay full price for a car!"[28] Spielberg called and cancelled his order and refused to change his mind even when the dealership's owner apologized.)

DIVORCE

These were not good years for the Spielberg family. The personality differences between Arnold and Leah finally took their toll, and the move to California capped it. Writer Alan Vanneman describes the breakdown as "a slow-motion spiral to disaster and divorce—long periods of silence and avoidance punctuated by bitter arguments that left Steven and his three younger sisters trembling."[29] There was also Leah Spielberg's relationship with Bernie Adler, Arnold's assistant at General Electric. When the Spielbergs separated in 1966, Arnold moved to Los Angeles. (On April 6, 1997, he married Bernice Colner.) Leah and the kids moved to Phoenix where she married Bernie in 1967. (Trivia: Marrying Adler took Leah back to her Orthodox roots. She and Bernie opened a kosher deli in Los Angeles called the Milky Way. Whenever her son is in town filming, she sends a "Tuna Stuffer" to him for lunch. He also loves the cabbage rolls.) The divorce was traumatic for Steven, which is why the topic occurs in so many of his movies. And though his parents and sisters adored him, Spielberg has said, "I always felt alone for some reason. My mom had her agenda, my dad his, my sisters theirs. *E.T.*, which certainly defines loneliness from my own perspective, is a lot about how I felt about my mom and dad when they finally got a divorce."[30]

UNIVERSAL STUDIOS

There is a story, supposedly perpetuated by Spielberg himself, that during a visit to Universal Studios he left the tourist tram and struck out on his own and then began going to the Universal lot every day. No one stopped him because he wore a suit, carried a briefcase, and adopted the air of someone who had the right to be there. For three months he hung around movie directors, writers, and editors. He even used an empty office and put his name and room number on the building's directory and gave his extension to the switchboard. Eventually, he was stopped and questioned by Chuck Silvers, assistant to the editorial supervisor for Universal TV.

The truth is that Steven's dad asked a friend to ask Chuck Silvers to show his son around the studio's postproduction offices. Silvers agreed and spent a day with Steven showing him around and talking with him about making movies. During the school year, the two corresponded, and Silvers gave the young man an unpaid job as a clerical assistant in the editorial department during the summers of 1964 and 1965. Instead of his own office, however, he shared a space with the company's purchasing agent and spent much of his time helping her with orders. He also made deliveries around the lot and took great advantage of it. Not only did he see Alfred Hitchcock, he ate lunch with Charlton Heston and Cary Grant. He spent much of his time in the editing rooms learning from the experts and even helped edit a popular television western. He soon became friends with Tony Bill, a young actor turned producer/director who showed interest in Spielberg's work. Bill introduced Spielberg to Francis Ford Coppola and took him to an acting class taught by actor/director John Cassavetes. "I got off on the right foot," says Spielberg, "learning how to deal with actors as I watched Cassavetes dealing with his repertory company."[31] He even worked as a production assistant on the Cassavetes film *Faces*.

After he graduated from Saratoga High School in 1965, Steven moved in with his father and applied to the film schools at the University of Southern California and to the University of California at Los Angeles, but both turned him down because of poor grades. He finally enrolled at California State College at Long Beach (CSLB), which had no film school but was located near Los Angeles and Universal Studios. (Spielberg is also honest enough to say that college was a way to evade the Vietnam draft.) It was around this time that he went to the Nuart and Vagabond theaters in Los Angeles and discovered many of the movies that he had not been allowed to see growing up. In fact, most of Spielberg's film education before and since has been from watching late-night movies on television. He arranged his classes so he could spend three days a week at Universal, but after awhile he attended so few classes that his father asked Silvers to encourage Steven to go to school. Silvers told the senior Spielberg that movie studios required only talent, not degrees. When Steven learned that producers would preview only 16mm or 35mm movies, he took a job in the college cafeteria to earn the money to buy a 16mm camera and film and then spent weekends making movies with college buddies as actors. In later years, his professors would remember him as the kid with cameras hanging around his neck who was always filming and writing. During the divorce and soon after, Arnold Spielberg and his son became close, both sharing their sadness, but it bothered Arnold that his son did not take education seriously. The two grew estranged again, and Steven moved into an apartment with a classmate.

BREAKING INTO THE BIG TIME

By 1967, Spielberg was ready to make his "calling-card film," the one he would show to Universal executives to prove he could handle a camera, lighting, and actors. *Slipstream* was a simple 35mm story about bicycle racing starring Tony Bill. Spielberg's roommate, Ralph Burris, wanted to become a movie producer and decided to let Spielberg's film be his spring-board, while Arnold Spielberg contributed equipment and financing. Serge Haginere and Allen Daviau, Spielberg's cameramen, spent week-ends in the desert and in Santa Monica filming racing footage from dif-ferent angles. Unfortunately, rain prevented the final weekend's shooting and time was up for the crane and equipment operators, so *Slipstream* had to be cancelled. But when Spielberg found another aspiring young pro-ducer who wanted to back a short film, he began working on *Amblin'* on July 4, 1968, with Daviau as director of photography and himself as writer and director. *Amblin'* is a simple story about a young man and woman who fall in and out of love as they hitchhike from California's desert to its ocean. Again, friends and family helped out with only a film credit as payment but, for a change, the film had nothing to do with Steven's child-hood. Only 26 minutes long, the movie scored big with Chuck Silvers and Sid Sheinberg, president of Universal Television, who offered Spielberg a $275/week seven-year contract to direct television programs with the chance of directing movies. Spielberg quit college without emptying his locker! (Note: On May 31, 2002, Spielberg graduated from California State University Long Beach with a bachelor's degree in film and elec-tronic arts. Wearing a cap and gown, he marched in the commencement ceremony with his fellow graduates, but when *he* crossed the stage, the band played the *Indiana Jones* theme music.)

But he had not read the contract before signing it and soon found that he was being paid for doing nothing, so he returned to Sheinberg and told him he wanted to work. Sheinberg called producer William Sackheim (known for guiding young talent) and told him to use Spielberg in the television se-ries *Night Gallery*. When the grateful young man asked Chuck Silvers how he could possibly repay him for contacting Sheinberg, Silvers told him to do two things: always help young moviemakers and always give him (Silvers) a hug each time they meet. Spielberg continues to keep those two promises. On December 12, 1968, the *Hollywood Reporter* announced, "Spielberg, 21, is believed to be the youngest filmmaker ever pacted by a major studio."[32]

NOTES

1. Quoted in Susan Goldman Rubin, *Steven Spielberg: Crazy for Movies* (New York: Harry N. Abrams, 2001), 9.

2. Quoted in Fred A. Bernstein, "Steven Spielberg's Mother. An Interview with Leah Adler," *The Jewish Mothers' Hall of Fame* (New York: Doubleday, 1986), www.fredbernstein.com/articles/.

3. Ibid.

4. Library of Congress, "Tribute to Mr. Arnold Spielberg," U.S. Senate, April 6, 2001, www.thomas.loc.gov/.

5. Quoted in John Baxter, *Steven Spielberg: The Unauthorised Biography* (London: HarperCollins, 1996), 20.

6. Quoted in Bernstein.

7. Quoted in Frank Sanello, *Spielberg: The Man, The Movies, The Mythology* (Dallas: Taylor, 1996), 118.

8. Margaret Downey, "Spielberg Finally Convinced to Leave BSA," *Scouting for All*, July 2, 2001, www.scoutingforall.org.

9. Quoted in Sanello, 9.

10. Quoted in Joseph McBride, *Steven Spielberg: A Biography* (New York: Simon and Schuster, 1997), 11.

11. Steve Poster, "The Mind Behind *Close Encounters of the Third Kind*," *American Cinematographer*, February 1978, reprinted in *Steven Spielberg Interviews*, Lester D. Friedman and Brent Notbohm, eds. (Jackson: University Press of Mississippi, 2000), 57.

12. Quoted in Rubin, 6.

13. Quoted in Tony Crawley, *The Steven Spielberg Story: The Man Behind the Movies* (New York: Quill, 1983), 16.

14. Quoted in Sanello, 20.

15. Quoted in Zac Champ, "The Steven Spielberg Directory," www.scruffles.net/ (accessed July 5, 2006).

16. Quoted in Crawley, 13.

17. Quoted in Champ.

18. Quoted in Crawley, 12.

19. Champ.

20. Quoted in Sanello, 4.

21. Quoted in Sanello, 6.

22. Quoted in CNN.com, "Hollywood's Master Storyteller. Steven Spielberg Profile," www.cnn.com/, accessed July 5, 2006.

23. Quoted in Poster, 59.

24. Quoted in Poster, 57.

25. Crawley, 16.

26. Quoted in Poster, 60.

27. Quoted in Sanello, 7.

28. Quoted in ibid.

29. Alan Vanneman, "Steven Spielberg: A Jew in America," *Bright Lights Film Journal*, August 2003, www.brightlightsfilm.com/, (accessed July 5, 2006).

30. Quoted in "Hollywood's Master Storyteller."

31. Quoted in Rubin, 25.

32. Quoted in Sanello, 28.

Chapter 2

FROM TV TO FILM, 1969–1977

PROFESSIONAL DIRECTING DEBUT: *NIGHT GALLERY*

Although Spielberg was anxious to make feature movies, he eagerly asked questions of everyone around him to learn as much as possible from television. His first assignment was an episode of *Night Gallery* titled "Eyes" starring film legend Joan Crawford. Movies made for television were introduced by Universal in 1964, and even today they are often pilots for prospective television series. *Night Gallery* was such a project. (It was also three rather spooky stories compacted into two hours.) Spielberg was thrilled to work on the series because of his admiration for its creator, writer, and host Rod Serling of *Twilight Zone* fame, but he was "terrified"[1] to direct Crawford, a woman who intimidated almost everyone. An actress since the early days of movies, Crawford was making her television debut. At first she disliked the idea of such a young director, but she soon relied on him much more, says Spielberg, that he expected. He was 21 and she was 65, but they soon became friends. Barry Sullivan was the actor in the movie and helped the young director when he could. To repay the kindness, Spielberg hired Sullivan twice in later years. When Spielberg asked Sheinberg if he could work on a project about younger people, he was told, "I'd take this opportunity if I were you."[2]

Work began on February 3, 1969. At first the crew did not take the young director seriously and thought he might be part of a publicity stunt, but that changed when they saw that he was always prepared and carried storyboards with him throughout the production. And though he disliked the script, he used his talent with the camera to make it more interesting. In his biography of the director, Frank Sanello writes that the *Night Gallery* episode is considered a "treasure trove" of Spielberg's "signature style of filmmaking," which he would "later perfect in his blockbusters and masterpiece: the use of wide-angle lenses, lots of dolly and crane shots, and dramatic lighting to maximize the overall visual impact."[3] And while zoom lenses were something new on the filmmaking scene, Spielberg preferred tracking shots so that the camera moved toward the actors. He also used some innovative cutting techniques. The show aired on NBC on November 8, 1969, to mixed reviews. While one reviewer criticized the director's youth, Joan Crawford told a reporter from the *Detroit Free Press*, "Go interview that kid because he's going to be the biggest director of all time."[4] But Spielberg believed that he had done an "awful job"[5] and took a leave of absence. During his time off, he wrote screenplays, but when none were accepted, he was ready to return to directing—even television. He directed episodes of *Marcus Welby, M.D.* (ABC), *Columbo* (NBC/ABC), *Name of the Game* (three series shown alternately) (NBC), *Owen Marshall, Counselor at Law* (ABC), and another episode of *Night Gallery*. He particularly enjoyed directing the first and last episodes of a short-lived series, *The Psychiatrist*, because he was allowed to give input and incorporate his own ideas. He is especially proud of an episode with Clu Gulager in which Gulager's character is a golfer dying of cancer whose golfing buddies come to visit him. It was Spielberg's idea to have the friends give Gulager a box in which they had placed the 18th hole with a flag in it. Gulager then improvised by squeezing the dirt on himself while tearfully telling his friends that it was the best gift he had ever received. Spielberg also enjoyed directing Peter Falk and watching the actor create his character in the pilot of *Columbo*, but soon he was so bored that he says he felt more passion making home movies.

BREAK-OUT TELEVISION MOVIE: *DUEL*

When Spielberg's feelings were so low that he began to reconsider his career choice, Universal bought the rights to *Duel*. Written by Richard Matheson, *Duel* is about David Mann, a traveling salesman who unknowingly angers a truck driver who first rides his tail then tries to kill him. Mann even stops and calls the police, but he cannot shake off the truck. When Spielberg read the script, he vividly remembered how *he* felt the first time he drove the Los Angeles freeways, and he persuaded the producers to let him direct it. Shooting began on September 13, 1971, in Soledad Canyon, California. Dennis Weaver had been on television in other roles and was currently in *McCloud* (NBC) playing a deputy marshal from Taos, New Mexico, who fights crime in New York City. But, according to the International Movie Database, it was Dennis Weaver's acting in *Touch of Evil* (1958) that convinced Spielberg that he would be perfect for the role of David Mann. Weaver, however, wanted his character to challenge the truck, but Spielberg convinced him that it was better that Mann be a fairly unconfident individual who would never consider such a challenge.

Spielberg also used a trick perfected by Alfred Hitchcock to create suspense: the fear of the unknown. Hitchcock once described this theory. "A bomb is under the table, and it explodes: That is surprise. The bomb is under the table but it does not explode: That is suspense."[6] Spielberg was also very careful to choose a truck with a bulkhead up front so it would hide the driver and make the truck seem driverless. He included smaller disconcerting incidents—such as keys falling out of locks—to show how technology was disrupting society. He actually wanted the movie to have no dialogue, but the producers vetoed the idea. Since the movie is about a chase, Spielberg made elaborate storyboards by having an artist make a map that looked as if a helicopter had photographed the entire chase route including scene indicators. The long mural was wrapped around Spielberg's hotel room, and he checked off scenes as they were filmed. Production ran over schedule by three days but stayed in the $3 million budget. It aired November 13, 1971, as an *ABC Movie of the Weekend* and earned very good reviews. While Spielberg received the biggest career boost—Cecil Smith of the *Los Angeles Times* dubbed the young director "the *wunderkind* of the film business"[7]—everyone connected with the movie profited with better earning power. The movie so impressed famed director David Lean, one of Spielberg's idols, that he is to have said, "Immediately I knew that here was a very bright new director."[8] With *Duel*, writes biographer Tony Crawley, Spielberg "literally changed the face, pace and close-cropped confines of the still infant TV-movie genre and helped mature it into an occasional art-form."[9] Two years later *Duel* was released as a feature film in Europe and made Spielberg a director "of immense potential in Europe."[10] Universal earned at least $6 million there and sent Spielberg on a publicity tour. Among the awards won by *Duel* and/or its director: "Special Mention" at the twelfth Monte Carlo Television Festival; Grand Prix of the first French Festival du Cinema Fantastique (January 1973); the jury's Gariddi a'Oro award as Best *Opera Prima* (first film) at Taormina's Festival in Italy (summer 1973); and the Picture-of-the-Month Trophy in West Germany. The Italians tried to get the young director to admit that the truck in *Duel* represented the "all-powerful, all-crushing forces of the capitalist Establishment"[11] but he would not agree. *Duel* was shown in American theaters in 1983. (Trivia: Only in the theatrical version can you see Spielberg in David Mann's backseat. He was giving directions to Dennis Weaver.) Spielberg says, "Television taught me how to be a professional within a very chaotic business."[12] Tony Crawley quotes Spielberg as saying that television "taught me to think on my feet. To plan my movies, do my homework, make sure I knew what I was doing every day before coming on the set."[13] As Crawley adds, Spielberg learned that television is about speed—quick work with no time for special shots. He also learned about cannibalism, the common practice of incorporating footage from other films; but when Spielberg learned that scenes from *Duel* were used in an episode of the television series *The Incredible Hulk* in 1978, he had all of his contracts rewritten, adding a clause to prevent it from happening to any of his films.

After *Duel*, Spielberg began shooting another made-for-television movie, *Something Evil*, for CBS. Darren McGavin and Sandy Dennis starred in the story about a couple moving into a haunted farmhouse. The film's photographer, Bill Butler, would later film *Jaws* for Spielberg, and Carl Gottlieb, who acted in the movie, would later help Spielberg write *Jaws*. Even Spielberg has a small part in the movie. The film aired January 21, 1972. Spielberg's next TV movie was *Savage* (aka *Watch Dog* aka *The Savage Report*). Another pilot for a television series, this show starred the husband and wife team Martin Landau and Barbara Bain, who had been very successful in *Mission Impossible* (CBS, 1973/ABC, 1989–1990). In *Savage* Landau plays a television reporter and Bain his producer. They try to uncover secrets on a nominated Supreme Court judge played by Barry Sullivan. The movie aired on March 31, 1973, on NBC, but was not picked up as a series. Steven Spielberg was only 25 but already concerned that he was being typecast as an "episodic director."[14] He was ready to make a feature film.

SPIELBERG'S FORGOTTEN MOVIE: *ACE ELI AND RODGER OF THE SKIES*

Spielberg had been sending his own stories and scripts to studios without any luck until producers David Brown and Richard D. Zanuck bought his story, *Ace Eli and Rodger of the Skies*, for 20th Century Fox. But the two men were soon fired because of the studio's big losses and replaced by Elmo Williams. When studios change production chiefs, they usually drop newly purchased projects, but Spielberg was fortunate that Williams kept his. Williams did not, however, want Spielberg to direct the movie. *Ace Eli and Rodger of the Skies* is a sweet old-fashioned movie set during the 1920s starring Cliff Robertson, Patricia Smith, and Eric Shea. Robertson plays a husband and father with dreams of being a barnstorming pilot traveling the country and taking people for rides in his plane. The movie, released in April 1973, received terrible reviews and made barely enough money to cover the costs. One wonders how much different it might have been had Spielberg directed it.

DIRECTING HIS FIRST FEATURE FILM: *THE SUGARLAND EXPRESS*

Brown and Zanuck thought highly of Spielberg and helped him direct his first feature film, *The Sugarland Express*. In May 1969, Spielberg read a newspaper article about a wife who helped her husband escape from prison. The two took a patrolman hostage and then led a massive high-speed chase as they attempted to retrieve their children from foster parents. In the story he developed with Hal Barwood and Matthew Robbins, Spielberg softened the characters to make them easier for audiences to accept. As he had done with *Duel*, he used a room-wrapping mural/storyboard with which to follow the route of the motorcade. He used toy cars to plan camera angles. There were 90 police cars in the real chase in Texas, but since his budget allowed for only 40, he used different techniques to add the extra 50 cars. He used natural lighting to give the feeling of a documentary and added more realism by using the real prison pre-release center near Sugarland, Texas. To shoot the cars while they were moving, he anchored the camera to a platform on a track. He was also able to film inside the police cars because of a new compact camera just developed by California's Panavision Corporation. When Spielberg's sister, Anne, visited the set, she found her brother filming from the roof of a chicken restaurant, and they silently acknowledged to each other that he had made it to the big leagues. (Trivia: Spielberg purchased the hijacked Texas Department of Public Safety patrol car and the revolving neon chicken sign that stood atop the restaurant.)

For his leading lady (Lou Jean Poplin), Spielberg chose Goldie Hawn, who had won an Academy Award for her supporting role in *Cactus Flower* in 1969 and was tremendously popular on the NBC television variety series *Rowan & Martin's Laugh-In*. William Atherton was chosen as her husband, Clovis Michael Poplin, and Ben Johnson was chosen to play Captain Harlin Tanner. To write the music, Spielberg chose John Williams—probably one of the best decisions he would ever make. Spielberg's lifelong love of movies includes movie music. In fact, when he and his sisters played their home version of *Name That Tune* (NBC, 1953–1954/CBS, 1954–1959), they often used movie soundtracks. Because of this, Spielberg was familiar with Williams's work, something that impressed the composer. In turn, Williams admired Spielberg for his memory, energy, vitality, and kindness. (The world is familiar with this dynamic duo, but many may wonder how they perform their magic. As Spielberg shows the film to Williams, he describes what music he thinks would be appropriate in which scenes. "But once Johnny sits down at the piano, it's his movie, it's his score. It's his original overdraft, a super-imposition."[15]) When *The Sugarland Express* opened on April 5, 1974, it received "outstanding reviews."[16] Pauline Kael of the *New Yorker* wrote, "This is one of the most phenomenal debut films in the history of movies."[17] The movie even won the Best Screenplay Award at the 1974 Cannes Film Festival. But good reviews and awards do not assure box-office success, and *The Sugarland Express* failed in that area. Some believed that the audience had a hard time seeing Goldie Hawn play a serious role. Whatever the reason, Spielberg promised himself that he would "hook"[18] the audience in his next film.

JAWS

Among Spielberg's numerous phobias and fears are water and the things hidden beneath its surface. What better way to overcome this fear than to make a film on the ocean about the sea's greatest killer and thereby pass on his fear to the audience? This was exactly his plan after reading Peter Benchley's novel *Jaws*. When a young girl is found killed by a shark off the coast of Amity, a coastal vacation town in New England, Mayor Larry Vaughn (Murray Hamilton) and Police Chief Martin Brody (Roy Scheider) argue about closing the beaches. Brody calls in shark expert Matt Hooper (Richard Dreyfuss) and shark hunter Quint (Robert Shaw) to find and kill the shark. (Spielberg originally wanted Jon Voight for Hooper and Lee Marvin for Quint.) Spielberg also hired Lorraine Gary to play Brody's wife, a decision that pleased her husband, Sid Sheinberg. Although producers David Brown and Richard D. Zanuck originally had another director in mind for the film, Spielberg begged for it. He knew right away that he wanted Roy Scheider to play Brody and that he wanted to give Brody his (Spielberg's) own fear of water. But that was just the beginning of how Spielberg entwined his personal life into the movie. His cocker spaniel, Elmer, is Brody's dog in the film. His father, Arnold, is one of the people on the beach. A little boy sings "Do You Know the Muffin Man?" which was one of Spielberg's favorite childhood songs. He also included a scene showing Boy Scouts working for their merit badges in swimming, and lastly, he used his favorite location, the suburbs, by showing ordinary people on vacation.

Benchley attempted two screenplays before Spielberg hired friend and screenwriter Carl Gottlieb. The two men rented a house on Martha's Vineyard so they could work on the script each night for the next day's shooting. This allowed for much improvisation from the cast, something Spielberg enjoys and encourages. In fact, much of *Jaws* was ad-libbed by the actors who met in Spielberg's house to rehearse. Production on the movie began on May 2, 1974, before there was even a script, a cast—or a shark. Spielberg hired Bob Mattey to build the shark, the same Bob Mattey who built the giant squid in the Walt Disney film *20,000 Leagues Under the Sea*. There were actually three sharks made. All three were named Bruce (Trivia: Bruce is Spielberg's lawyer's name), and all three were divas. Bruce #1 sank. Bruce #2 exploded. Bruce #3 filmed the movie but was extremely uncooperative. His eyes crossed and his jaws did not always close correctly. But Spielberg is an expert at making lemonade out of lemons and made a better film because of Bruce's foul nature by using the Alfred Hitchcock trick he had previously used in *Duel:* the *threat* of the shark. He knew that the threat would create more suspense than would too many appearances of a mechanical shark. It certainly worked, especially when coordinated with the shark's theme music, now as internationally recognizable as that of the shower scene music in Hitchcock's *Psycho*. Even when the shark strikes, the audience often sees the character's reaction and/or the damage inflicted instead of the shark itself. In *Jaws* there are occasions when the camera is on Brody's face as he sees, or thinks he sees, something happening or about to happen. In those scenes, the audience takes its cue from Brody. There are even some false alarms, but false alarms work to placate the audience, thus leaving them easier to scare. In his book *The Great Movies II*, Roger Ebert writes about one of the scenes that adds suspense. While Brody is looking at books on sharks, the audience is looking over his shoulder at "page after page of fearsome teeth, cold little eyes, and victims with chunks taken out of their bodies." Spielberg, writes Ebert, is "establish[ing] the killer in our minds."[19] The director's favorite scene is one of the most haunting and one that makes the shark even more frightening, yet the shark is nowhere to be seen. The three main characters are sitting in the boat's cabin drinking, comparing scars, laughing, and telling stories. But the cabin turns deathly quiet when Quint starts telling the others about being a sailor on the USS *Indianapolis* when the ship sank at the end of World War II. Those who survived the sinking floated for days without food or water. Surrounded by sharks, he saw one friend after another pulled under and wondered if he would be next.

Years later Spielberg watched *Jaws* and said that it was "the simplest movie I had ever seen in my life. It was just the essential moving, working parts of suspense and terror, with just enough character development that at one point in the movie you hate Schieder and you hate Shaw and you hate Dreyfuss . . . then you like them again."[20] The movie, he says, was "all content [and] experiment."[21] Richard Dreyfuss recalls the filming being the most "intense"[22] of his career. It was also intense for Spielberg, who not only almost quit, he was almost drowned, was almost crushed between two boats, and was almost chewed up by a propeller. As for filming, the weather and water changed so often that it was hard to match shots from one day to the next, and when Spielberg wanted the three main characters to appear to be far out and alone in the ocean, tourists brought their boats by to watch. In the scene where the boat's cabin fills with water, Roy Scheider so feared a real accident that he took his own axe and hammer in case he had to free himself. To top it off, Zanuck and Brown wanted to use real sharks. Cast and crew became anxious to go home and some began calling the film "Flaws."[23] Spielberg says that "four days out of seven"[24] he was sure he was making a "turkey,"[25] and he feared that his once-promising career was already finished. There were even rumors that Universal executives were threatening to cancel production. Had it not been for what they saw in each day's raw footage, they might have. No one had taken a film 100 days over schedule, especially a director whose first film had failed at the box office. There were many days when Spielberg sat in the boat waiting for a scene to be ready and thinking that he was wasting time and effort and that his vision could not be realized. It was during those moments that he swore he would never again film on water.

Thankfully, he habitually overshoots so his editors always have more than enough film to work with. This gave the editor of *Jaws*, Verna Fields, the ability to put together a terrific movie. But Spielberg is a perfectionist and known for "tinkering,"[26] so even though the preview audiences rated the movie higher than 99 percent, there was a part of the movie that Spielberg felt dragged a bit. Cast and crew went to Verna Fields's home and filled her swimming pool with powdered milk to make the water look murky as it does off of Martha's Vineyard. He added a sunken rowboat and had a corpse's head pop out of it thus making one of the most frightening scenes in the movie.

Steven's sister, Anne, sat with him at the special screening for distributors who, she says, usually sit "stone-faced."[27] That night, however, they "were going wild."[28] On a personal level, she saw the movie as a rite of passage for their family. "For years he [Spielberg] just scared us. Now he gets to scare the masses."[29] Richard Dreyfuss was similarly surprised at the film's premier in New York City (June 1975) when Spielberg received a standing ovation and the crowd responded to the movie with cheers and applause, something he had never witnessed. The reaction was the same everywhere, and the movie broke all box-office records. Only two weeks after its release, *Jaws* became the most successful movie in history up to that time and the first to reach the $100 million mark. More than 67 million Americans went to see it that first summer. Roger Ebert writes that *Jaws* "is one of the most effective thrillers ever made."[30] The movie created a fear of sharks comparable to the fear of showers created by *Psycho*. It became the first summer "blockbuster"[31] and made summer *the* movie season. At first, Spielberg thought it was a "fluke,"[32] but later he said, "I realized we made a movie that was just super-intense and somehow struck a chord around the world."[33] *Jaws* had immediately become the epitome of the adventure movie and the goal for which all future adventure movies still strive. Its characters were each totally different, yet they all "held their own with the shark."[34] In 2006, the movie was named the number one "When Animals Attack" film by the *Sydney Morning Herald*.

The movie was nominated in the Best Motion Picture category at the Academy Awards, and editor Fields and composer Williams each went home with an Oscar. Each of the three main actors—Dreyfuss, Scheider, and Shaw—became hot properties, but Steven Spielberg became "the hottest property in Hollywood."[35] As always, there were some people who believed that he had peaked and who jealously called the movie "commercial drivel."[36] *Jaws* continues to have a hold on the world's population, and it is impossible to find a mention of summer movies without it. An inaugural *Jaws* Fest was held in Martha's Vineyard, Massachusetts, for a week beginning June 3, 2005. The chamber of commerce made the area look like Amity Island and planned numerous events. The timing coincided with the release of the thirtieth-anniversary edition of the movie, which was shown on a beachside screen. The book's author, Peter Benchley, was among the more than 2,000 people who attended. Spielberg was there via a videotaped introduction to the movie. He was, and is, quick to give much of the credit for the movie's success to John Williams.

When Benchley died in February 2006, Spielberg credited him with a project that was so successful that it gave him artistic freedom in his movies. But with the success of *Jaws*, not only did he have artistic freedom, he had plenty of money. While he told a reporter that he was now worth $4 million, he did not include the money made from a recently updated contract that his agent, Guy McElwaine, had renegotiated before *Jaws* so that Spielberg would receive an additional 5 percent profit. As Sanello writes, "tens of millions of dollars in excess of the paltry $4 million."[37] But how did he spend the money? Buying cars and dating starlets? His production editor for *Close Encounters of the Third Kind*, Julia Phillips, writes that

Spielberg did enjoy driving around theaters showing *Jaws* to take pictures of the long lines. "He is so blatant in his excitement for himself," she writes, "that his is adorable."[38] And he did attract his fair share of groupies and girls. "After *Jaws*," says the director, "I did cut loose a little. I only went a little crazy because I was too busy to become a real hedonist."[39] Among others, he dated Victoria Principal and Sarah Miles, but he says that he did not actively seek out women and parties. He kept the same car and the same house and did not take the time to travel or pursue spending his money. In fact, he was spending some of his time with the businessmen of Hollywood learning about distribution. And he did not hesitate when asked to speak to a UCLA film class. He took no bodyguards or entourage, just his good friend and director, Brian De Palma. They arrived before the teacher and waited in the hallway until he arrived. The "hottest property in Hollywood"[40] told students how he directed a few scenes, but he also told them that success was a lot of luck and being prepared for when that luck finds you. He had been ready, he told them, since he was 18.

CLOSE ENCOUNTERS OF THE THIRD KIND

How would you top *Jaws?* Steven Spielberg turned to aliens. Many years ago Arnold Spielberg told his young son that if aliens exist, he thinks they are friendly and visit earth to share knowledge. This is probably why *Close Encounters of the Third Kind* introduced friendly aliens, not the horrifyingly cruel ones shown in movies made in the 1950s. "I have tried," Spielberg says, "to take interspace relationships out of the science fiction closet and give them an aura of respectability."[41] He also wanted audiences to think about their relationship with the universe. The movie was inspired by Spielberg's childhood movie, *Firelight,* and the Disney song, "When You Wish upon a Star," from *Pinocchio.* "I pretty much hung my story on the mood the song created, the way it affected me emotionally,"[42] he says. He was still filming *Jaws* in 1974 when he got the idea for *Close Encounters,* and his script for it "was stalled"[43] at Columbia, because he could not get the $12 million he needed to make it. After the release of *Jaws* in 1975, he could get whatever he wanted. One of the images most identified with *Close Encounters* is a little boy looking out a big open door. The image, says Spielberg, sums up his work. What is outside that door? Promise or danger? Since this was his first entry into science fiction, he credits much of the movie's believability to Dr. J. Allen Hynek, his technical adviser. Hynek was a nonbeliever of unidentified flying objects (UFOs) who studied accounts and became a believer. It is he who developed the three levels of encounter: visible sighting, physical evidence, and contact. Is

Spielberg a believer? He says that there are just too many people with believable experiences to ignore. He does, however, believe more in the second form of contact than the third.

Close Encounters of the Third Kind is about several people who see a UFO and then find themselves drawn to Devil's Tower in Wyoming, where they meet friendly aliens. Richard Dreyfuss knew right away that he wanted to play the main character, Roy Neary, but Spielberg wanted Steve McQueen. McQueen liked the script but said he could not cry on film. When Spielberg said he would cut the crying out of the movie, McQueen told him that it should be left in the movie but he could not do it. Dustin Hoffman, Al Pacino, and Gene Hackman also turned down the role; James Caan said he would make it for $1 million upfront and 10 percent of the gross. In the meantime, Richard Dreyfuss was actively campaigning for the role. When he reminded Spielberg that Neary should be childlike and that he, Dreyfuss, *was* the "everyman" actor that Spielberg prefers, Spielberg relented. "Richard's so wound up in a kind of kinetic energy. He's as close an actor to Spencer Tracy as exists today. I also think he represents the underdog in all of us."[44] Spielberg appreciates actors like Dreyfuss "who will go out on a limb, even to the point of embarrassing himself, to be different, to do something unusual, to not be Richard Dreyfuss, but to be the person that the writer intended him to be."[45] One of the actresses who read for the role of Neary's wife was Meryl Streep. Although she was not a big star at the time, she already had a presence that intimidated both Dreyfuss and Spielberg. Teri Garr got the role after Spielberg saw her in a coffee commercial and thought that she *was* the everyday housewife. Melinda Dillon was cast on a Thursday and expected on the set the following Monday. The little boy, Cary Guffey, who had no acting experience, was chosen when the casting director saw him in his niece's daycare center. Since the three-year-old usually completed his scenes in just one take, Spielberg had a T-shirt made for him with his new nickname on it: "One-Take Cary."[46] Perhaps the biggest casting coup for Spielberg was getting one of his idols, French director Francois Truffaut, whose participation, says Spielberg, added more class and nobility to the movie. And, of course, after John Williams's huge success with the magical notes for the shark's theme in *Jaws*, Spielberg asked him to do it again for *Close Encounters*. He wanted earthlings and aliens to communicate with lights, colors, and music—a specific five notes of music. (Two bits of Trivia: Spielberg actually re-edited the movie to match Williams's score; and Spielberg's dog was with the humans when they were released from the mother ship.)

Spielberg used storyboards and 65mm film to maintain picture quality for the special effects. He chose Douglas Trumbull for his special visual effects director because Trumbull had worked on *2001: A Space Odyssey*, a

1968 science fiction movie that has become a cult classic with science fiction aficionados. He chose Vilmos Zsigmond, the cinematographer he used on *Sugarland Express*, to be the director of photography. Spielberg also used a new device, a digital live-action recording system that locks the camera's movements into a disc for reuse. As with *Jaws*, *Close Encounters* was not without its share of problems. It took six attempts to find the right screenplay, five months to film, and one year to edit due to the more than 350 special effects. (The editing process takes usually about half that time.) Another problem was finding a soundstage that was large enough. They finally located a dirigible hangar in Alabama. Richard Dreyfuss wanted 5 percent of gross earnings but was talked out of the demand by producer Julia Phillips. Spielberg insisted on tight security so television producers could not make a quick rip-off of the idea. Lastly, it was hard for Spielberg to release his hold on the film because he always finds areas to improve, but he was forced to get the movie ready for release before he was satisfied because financially strapped Columbia Pictures needed a Christmas hit. Of course, there were those who predicted that the movie would flop, and *Vogue* magazine even wrote it up as, "preposterous, trivial, simple-minded, shallow, and steeped in pretension."[47] On the other hand, the *New Republic*'s Stanley Kauffmann wrote that it was, "breathtaking, stunning, dazzling, moving, and brilliant," and "one of the most overpowering, sheerly cinematic experiences I can remember."[48] Opening in November 1977, *Close Encounters of the Third Kind* was a huge success and, as *Time* reviewer Frank Rich wrote, it was proof that Spielberg's reputation "is no accident."[49] Spielberg received his first Best Director Academy Award nomination for *Close Encounters* but lost to Woody Allen for *Annie Hall*. Years later, he said that *Close Encounters* is the one film that dates him, that he can see how much he has changed and how optimistic and naïve he was then. He can no longer be the dreamer he used to be because he has seven children who must be raised in the practical world. And would he do what Roy Neary does in the movie, leave his family for the chance of a lifetime? No way. Carina Chocano writes for the *Los Angeles Times* that *Close Encounters* and *Jaws* are "marked by a sly baby-boomer antiestablishmentarianism that is hard to imagine him [Spielberg] embracing now."[50]

NOTES

1. Quoted in Frank Sanello, *Spielberg: The Man, The Movies, The Mythology* (Dallas: Taylor, 1996), 30.

2. Quoted in Tony Crawley, *The Steven Spielberg Story: The Man Behind the Movies* (New York: Quill, 1983), 21.

3. Sanello, 32.

4. Quoted in Sanello, 31.

5. Ibid.

6. Quoted in Roger Ebert, *The Great Movies II* (New York: Broadway Books, 2005), 204.

7. Quoted in Susan Goldman Rubin, *Steven Spielberg: Crazy for Movies* (New York: Harry N. Abrams, 2001), 32.

8. Ibid.

9. Crawley, 23.

10. Crawley, 23–24.

11. Crawley, 24.

12. Quoted in Sanello, 38.

13. Quoted in Crawley, 22–23.

14. Quoted in Crawley, 29.

15. Quoted in Mitch Tuchman, "Close Encounter with Steven Spielberg." *Film Comment*, January–February 1978, reprinted in *Steven Spielberg Interviews*, Lester D. Friedman and Brent Notbohm, eds. (Jackson: University Press of Mississippi, 2000), 50.

16. Rubin, 35.

17. Quoted in Rubin, 35.

18. Rubin, 35.

19. Ebert, 206.

20. Quoted in Richard Combs, "Primal Scream." *Sight and Sound,* Spring 1977, reprinted in *Steven Spielberg Interviews*, Lester D. Friedman and Brent Notbohm, eds. (Jackson: University Press of Mississippi, 2000), 36.

21. Ibid.

22. Quoted in Rubin, 39.

23. Ibid.

24. Ibid.

25. Ibid, 39.

26. Sanello, 53.

27. Quoted in Rubin, 41.

28. Ibid.

29. Ibid.

30. Ebert, 204.

31. International Movie Database, "Trivia for *Jaws*" (1975), www.imdb.com (accessed September 22, 2005).

32. Quoted in Susan Royal, "Steven Spielberg in His Adventure on Earth." *American Premiere*, July 1982, reprinted in *Steven Spielberg Interviews*, Lester D. Friedman and Brent Notbohm, eds. (Jackson: University Press of Mississippi, 2000), 98–99.

33. Ibid.

34. Quoted in Peter Biskind, "A World Apart." *Premiere*, May 1997, reprinted in *Steven Spielberg Interviews*, Lester D. Friedman and Brent Notbohm, eds. (Jackson: University Press of Mississippi, 2000), 198–199.

35. Sanello, 57.

36. Sanello, 55.

37. Sanello, 58.

38. Quoted in Sanello, 57.

39. Ibid.

40. Sanello, 57.

41. Sanello, 64.

42. Quoted in Rubin, 44.

43. Sanello, 63.

44. Quoted in Tuchman, 50.

45. Quoted in Steve Poster, "The Mind Behind *Close Encounters of the Third Kind*," *Steven Spielberg Interviews*, Lester D. Friedman and Brent Notbohm, eds. (Jackson: University Press of Mississippi, 2000), 63.

46. International Movie Database, "Trivia for *Close Encounters of the Third Kind* (1977)," www.imdb.com (accessed September 22, 2005).

47. Quoted in Sanello, 72.

48. Ibid.

49. Quoted in Rubin, 45.

50. Carina Chocano, "Movies: The Director's Art; To think like the masters; For Steven Spielberg, it takes a vicious alien attack to restore Dad as the head of the family." *Los Angeles Times*, July 10, 2005, E1. www.proquest.umi.com.

Chapter 3

DIRECTOR/PRODUCER, 1978–1983

FIRST PRODUCING PROJECT: *I WANNA HOLD YOUR HAND*

According to author Tony Crawley's book about Spielberg published in 1983, the success of *Jaws*—both by Spielberg and editor Verna Fields—put Universal Studios in the mood to give new directors their big break. In his lifelong promise to help young filmmakers, Spielberg decided to help University of Southern California (USC) graduates Robert Zemeckis (director) and Bob Gale (writer/partner) by choosing their script, *I Wanna Hold Your Hand*, to be the first movie he would produce. Universal's production chief, Ned Tanen, agreed to the project, but only if Spielberg promised to take over the directing duties if Zemeckis proved unable. Tanen also wanted Nancy Allen and Susan Kendall Newman in the film. (Allen is the former wife of director Brian De Palma, and Newman is the actress/producer daughter of Paul Newman.) Released in April 1978, the movie is a light-hearted look at the way the Beatles affected teenagers in 1964 in their first visit to the United States. The movie lost more money than any Universal film in three years. According to author Crawley, neither original nor new Beatles fans seemed to care.

THE BOMB: *1941*

With two huge hits under his belt, some say that Spielberg had a right to make a bomb, which he did. True, *The Sugarland Express* had not done well at the box office, but it had been well received by critics. In the case of *1941*, however, neither the box office nor critics had much good to say. Perhaps it was a bad year for movies. Francis Ford Coppola, Michael Cimino, and John Landis were all being berated for their movies *Apocalypse Now*, *Heaven's Gate*, and *Blues Brothers* respectively. The plot of Spielberg's movie was based in reality. After the Japanese attack on Pearl Harbor, the city of Los Angeles thought it had been invaded by the Japanese. In fact, in February 1942, a Japanese submarine *had* surfaced off the coast of Santa Barbara and fired missiles, all of which missed, at the Richfield Oil Refinery. Two nights later, a Japanese surveillance plane flew over Los Angeles. It is easy to see why the city became alarmed. It is also easy to see why some of the events might make good comedy, such as the civil defense wardens shooting out porch lights and neon signs. This is what Zemeckis and Gale thought after they read about the events in old newspapers. Executive producer and director John Milius described it as "a multi-million-dollar Three Stooges movie"[1] and says that he could find no one to buy the script. Eventually, he gave the project to Spielberg, who had wanted to make a comedy for a long time. Spielberg was also in the mood for something lighthearted after *Close Encounters of the Third Kind*. When he read the script by Zemeckis and Gale, he said it was like reading a *MAD* magazine. He liked the nuttiness of the time "when we all lost our minds, thought we were being invaded by Japanese commandos, [and] spent every last bullet shooting at clouds for eight hours straight . . . . I just laughed myself sick."[2] MGM owned the rights to the project, but Spielberg did not want to work for them, so he took the project to Universal Studios, who did not want to put up the needed $20 million. That quickly changed, however, when studio heads saw the dailies of *Close Encounters* and realized that they were about to have a megahit. Universal then agreed to co-finance *1941* with Columbia Studios. But even as he began the project, Spielberg says that his inner voice was warning him against it. He knew that comedy was hard to perfect and that he had no experience with it. Chris Hodenfield was a writer for *Rolling Stone* in 1980 when he interviewed Spielberg about *1941*. In his opinion, Spielberg left behind the art of suspense, put in too many characters, and moved the film along too quickly. It was a steady and continuous "slam-bang," he writes, with no "slow burn, the double take, the dreadful anticipation, the witty rejoinder."[3] Making movies, says Spielberg, is an unnatural business, almost like fighting a war with the director as the commanding officer. In the case of *1941*, he admits that he was not able to control his troops, that most of the actors wanted to be as crazy as stars John Belushi and Dan Ackroyd. Spielberg took full blame for the movie's failure but added, "If we don't take chances, we never learn how to fail."[4] The movie needed $70 million to break even, and in the year 1979–1980, it brought in $90 million. After making so much money for the studios with *Jaws* and *Close Encounters*, Spielberg was offended that the studio heads publicly criticized *1941* after the sneak preview, and he made no movies for them for three years. There was one reviewer who enjoyed the movie. David Denby of *New York* magazine wrote: "He's made a celebration of the gung-ho silliness of old war movies, a celebration of the Betty Grable/Betty Hutton period of American pop culture."[5]

RAIDERS OF THE LOST ARK

As a child unable to see movies as often as he wanted, Steven Spielberg made up for lost time every chance he got and, like most boys, could not get enough of serials such as *Commando Cody*. George Lucas also loved the old serials. The two men were in Hawaii when they got the idea to capture that youthful excitement, enthusiasm, and intensity by making an action-adventure movie "with a cliffhanger every second."[6] They differed, however, on what type of characters and setting they wanted. Spielberg wanted a James Bond–type, but Lucas wanted "to make a homage to Saturday matinee serials"[7] but also something with a supernatural sense. They combined their ideas, and Indiana Jones, a professor of archaeology, was born. But Jones is not a superhero and often gets into trouble, thus lending humor to the movie. Spielberg and Lucas had also decided that they would make a three-movie series, and perhaps a fourth movie. (Trivia: (1) Jones is named after Lucas's malamute, Indiana, who was also the prototype for Chewbacca in *Star Wars*; (2) Indiana's original last name was Smith.) The two men had the basic plot down in three days and then gave it to Lawrence Kasdan to write. The first of the series was titled *Raiders of the Lost Ark*. Its plot? "Indy" is hired by the United States to find the Ark of the Covenant before the Nazis do. The ark is valuable because its contents, the original Ten Commandments, are alleged to have amazing powers. Paramount's Michael Eisner was the only studio executive willing to take the risk after the failure of *1941*, believing that Spielberg would not fail twice.

As always, Spielberg wanted lesser-known actors, and his first choices were Amy Irving and Harrison Ford. But he and Amy had just broken up, so he hired Karen Allen. Lucas vetoed Ford because he had already featured the actor in *American Graffiti* (1973) and *Star Wars* (1977). Lucas liked Ford; he just did not want the same actor in all of his movies. Tom Selleck was chosen, but the filming dates interfered with his contract to star in CBS's *Magnum, P.I.* (1980–1988), so Ford was hired. Spielberg and

Allen disagreed about her character. Spielberg saw her as a "damsel in distress" while Allen saw her as someone much tougher. Allen once told a magazine writer that Steven Spielberg "is the kind of director who plans it all out in his head and the people he works with are just there to fulfill his plan."[8] Although she later tried to take back her words, Spielberg never hired her again (although it is rumored that she may appear in the fourth Indiana Jones movie). Casting Director Mike Fenton said that he would never again send Spielberg anyone with an ego because Spielberg "doesn't have an ego, and he just doesn't have time for that sort of thing."[9]

Filming began in Tunisia in North Africa in 1980 with London as the home base. Spielberg, Lucas, and Ford enjoy working together, and Spielberg is quick to say how much he learns from Lucas, especially about saving money with "creative shortcuts, how to give an audience an eyeful with *illusions* [sic] of grandeur."[10] One example is wanting 2,000 extras but achieving the same effect with 700 extras, miniatures in the background, and a wide-angle lens. "He makes working fun," says Ford about Spielberg. "He's so secure about what he's doing."[11] But things were not always pleasant. For one thing, Spielberg had to disregard his phobia of snakes, because there were thousands of them. More seriously, most of the cast were plagued by stomach ailments caused by living in a foreign country. Harrison Ford suffered horribly, so much in fact that it created the humor in the now-classic scene where Indy declines to fight with the large man wielding a saber. Because Ford desperately needed to hurry things along, he asked Spielberg how they could do so, and the director jokingly answered that Indiana could just shoot the man, so that is what he did. According to the bonus material in *The Adventures of Indiana Jones* DVD set, almost everyone got sick during the filming, and the heat was so intense that it was hard to breath. To take care of himself, Spielberg ate only canned foods from Britain.

In his book, *The Great Movies II*, Roger Ebert describes *Raiders* as nonstop action, villains, exotic locales, dangerous and yucky animals, reptiles, danger, humor, guns, spiders, magic, whips, and machetes. He also writes that the movie gave Spielberg a chance to "stick it to the Nazis"[12] and that Nazi symbols are destroyed throughout the movie. (Trivia: (1) The submarine used in the movie is the same one used in *Das Boot*, along with the World War II submarine pen and Nazi insignia; (2) the trick coat hanger was Spielberg's idea.) The boulder, which weighed 300 pounds and was 12 feet high, almost crushed Harrison Ford in one of the 10 takes.

In addition to teaching Spielberg how to control movie costs, Lucas helped Spielberg become a better businessman in other ways. "I personally would have never been so audacious," Spielberg says. "George made me realize what I deserved."[13] After the studio earned back its production costs, it earned 60 percent of the gross up to the first $100 million. After that, the studio split the earnings 50-50 with Lucas and Spielberg. Had the movie failed, Lucas still would have received $4 million for his producer's fees and Spielberg would have earned $1.5 million for director's fees. The movie finished ahead of schedule and under budget, and as of 1996, it grossed $363 million. Although Eisner's colleagues had been "furious"[14] when he made the original deal, they were certainly happy afterward, because *Raiders* made their stockholders $187 million in one week. There were still, of course, those who said that Spielberg's movies were "big on plot, but short on character,"[15] but most critics agreed with *Time* magazine's Richard Schickel, who writes, "so strong is the imagery, so compelling the pace, so sharply defined are the characters, that one leaves . . . with the feeling that, like the best films of childhood, it will take up permanent residence in memory."[16] Schickel also writes that *Raiders* is, "an object lesson in how to blend the art of storytelling with the highest levels of technical know-how, planning, cost control and commercial acumen."[17] Spielberg sees *Raiders* as a salute to the old serials without putting them down. "All the humor in the movie had to come from the characters, not the situation," and he admits that his villains were "cardboard Nazis."[18]

POLTERGEIST

Probably the most interesting Spielberg producing story is about *Poltergeist*, the ghost movie that Spielberg had wanted to make since he was a child. "*Poltergeist* is what I fear," he says, "and *E.T.* is what I love. One is about suburban evil and the other is about suburban good." He adds, "I had different motivations in both instances: In *Poltergeist* I wanted to terrify and I also wanted to amuse—I tried to mix the laughs and the screams together."[19] He also included his own fears of clowns and trees outside windows. Spielberg wrote and produced the movie but did not direct it. He offered that job to Tobe Hooper, the director of the cult classic, *The Texas Chain-Saw Massacre,* which Spielberg loves. Unfortunately for Hooper, it was to the studio's advantage to promote the film as a Spielberg movie, and, according to author Frank Sanello, Spielberg did not do much to repudiate it. He did the casting, which is usually left to the director, and he proudly insists that he was the "hands-on producer."[20] He says, "That was my production. I was very involved from the beginning."[21] Frank Marshall co-produced the movie and calls Spielberg the "creative force"[22] behind it. To make matters worse, the star of the movie, Craig

T. Nelson, publicly stated that Hooper "had not been allowed into the editing room."[23] Hooper was in a quandary. As Sanello writes, *Poltergeist* was the number-two film of the summer, and that is something an up-and-coming director definitely wants on his resume. But how do you argue with Steven Spielberg? The question was finally taken to the Directors Guild, and Tobe Hopper was declared the director. As for the editing, Hooper told Sanello, "I was in the editing room for ten weeks. There's very little difference between my cut and Steven's. I like the final cut very much . . . . The differences were just too minor."[24] Spielberg later took out a full-page ad in *Daily Variety* to send Hooper a letter complimenting his directing and thanking him for allowing him, Spielberg, so much leeway with the production. The letter, according to Sanello, was "part of a secret Directors Guild settlement that allowed Spielberg's name to be featured in movie trailers in letters twice as big as Hooper's. That plus $15,000."[25]

E.T. THE EXTRA-TERRESTRIAL

By the time of the completion of *Raiders*, Spielberg felt that he had lost the reason he wanted to make movies. He had always enjoyed stories about relationships, and he realized that once again he had been sucked into action-adventure. That would change with *E.T. the Extra-Terrestrial*, the movie to which Spielberg has said he most relates. There are two different stories about how/when the movie was conceived. One states that during an especially lonely time in his life, Spielberg wanted someone to talk with who needed him as much as he needed him or her. The other story is that he got the idea when filming the scene in *Close Encounters* when the spaceship's door closes. Both theories lead to the same resulting thought: What if one of the creatures in *Close Encounters* was left behind and became the friend of a lonely little boy on earth? The little boy took on aspects of Spielberg's childhood: a lonely boy who felt left out and had siblings he sometimes fought with and parents who got divorced. (He even included a scene in which the star, Elliott, releases frogs in science class— something Spielberg did when he was in school.) The director wanted a special friend to help the little boy get through these rough spots in his life. He wanted a child's vision with the least possible amount of adult interaction. The family lived in a ranch house in a suburban neighborhood because Spielberg grew up in such a neighborhood and because he sees suburbia as the place where the territories between children and adults are most distinguished. Where else can children hide secrets, and what bigger secret to hide than a friend from outer space? Spielberg shared these ideas with screenwriter Melissa Mathison, whose script for *The Black Stallion* he had enjoyed. Before she began writing the script in October 1980, she asked a group of children what powers they think an alien should have. She was surprised at two of their answers—the powers of telekinesis and healing—so she gave those powers to Elliott and E.T. Their psychic connection is exemplified in the movie when E.T. gets drunk while alone at home and Elliott acts as if he is drunk when he is away at school and has not been drinking. Spielberg sold the idea to Universal even while he was editing *Raiders,* and by the time he lost his second Best Director Oscar, he was filming it. Although he believes that storyboards and rehearsals are necessities for action movies, he also believes that they can stifle intimate movies and the spontaneity of children. He even shot the movie in sequence to make it seem real—as if the events really were unfolding to everyone. This made the actors bond more tightly to their fellow actors and to the story, so much so that when E.T. is dying and when he leaves, the cast and crew were really heartbroken.

But a month before shooting there was still no Elliott. Spielberg just could not find the right child. Producer Kathleen Kennedy says that you can almost tell if a child is right for a part when the child enters the room. There is something in their carriage and character that does or does not fit the role. They heard about 11-year-old Henry Thomas from Jack Fisk, who had directed Thomas in *Raggedy Man.* When Thomas's first reading with Spielberg did not go well, the director told him to think about his dog dying. Thomas was superb and even cried in the scene. According to legend, Spielberg said, "Okay, kid, you got the part!"[26] (Trivia: Thomas ad-libbed the scene with his toys and E.T. after he was given the direction to "introduce" the toys to the alien.) Drew Barrymore, Spielberg's goddaughter, had auditioned for *Poltergeist,* which Spielberg produced in 1982. While she was not right for that movie, Spielberg kept her in mind for something else, which turned out to be *E.T.* Evidently, Barrymore wove intricate and expressive stories to the director, which fit the personality of Gertie. As for the older brother, Michael, Spielberg says that Robert Mac-Naughton, who had previous stage experience, was the anchor to the family. Peter Coyote's clumsiness had lost him the role of Indiana Jones, but Spielberg wanted the trait for the role of "Keys" in *E.T.* Lastly, Dee Wallace Stone was chosen as the children's mother. The roles of adults were to be very low-key, but Stone was so much like a kid herself that her presence helped, rather than hurt, that feeling. According to Stone, "Steven is a master at casting. He watches people and has a real talent for taking their quality and putting them in the role that's right for them."[27] Eighteen years later the entire cast reunited to celebrate the release of the newly edited DVD, and Henry Thomas (Elliott) and Drew Barrymore (Gertie) recalled the director's methods. Thomas remembered pep talks before each scene and playing video games during breaks. Barrymore remembered Spielberg's gentle way of talking to her when she needed to cry in a scene. Although Dee Wallace Stone seemed to have only good memories at the reunion, several years before she had had some critical things to say about the making of the movie. Spielberg, she says, was obsessed with secrecy before the movie's release and even made everyone sign a promise not to divulge anything about it. She was also disappointed that she was not only refused star billing but was left out of the movie's advertisements. When Stone's career did not fare well after *E.T.*, she was asked if she had been blacklisted by Spielberg. She declined to comment.

The character of E.T. was, like Bruce in *Jaws*—three different E.T.s. Unlike Bruce, however, all three of the E.T.s worked. They were made by Carlo Rambaldi, the same man who made the alien puppet for *Close Encounters*. One E.T. could walk by itself; one could show facial expressions; and one was a suit worn by short actors. To allow for E.T.'s cables, interior sets were built on 10-foot elevated floors. Spielberg credits his director of photography, Allen Daviau, not only with making E.T. come alive but with making E.T. loveable and believable. Daviau accomplished this by making sure that E.T. was never shown in harsh lighting. And finally, John Williams added his magic with his now-recognizable score. M&Ms were the candy of choice in the movie when Elliott entices E.T., but the Mars company turned down the offer. The Hershey Food Company had just introduced Reese's Pieces and gladly lent their product to the movie. The result? Sales for the new candy increased by 65 percent when the movie came out. (Trivia: In the original version, police carried guns. Spielberg so disliked the image that he used computer graphics to delete the weapons for the movie's re-release.)

E.T. the Extra-Terrestrial premiered at the Cannes Film Festival in France in May 1982. Kathleen Kennedy said, "You couldn't even hear the end of the movie because people were on their feet stomping and yelling. And this huge searchlight started to sweep the top balcony to find us, and Steven stood up. It was one of the most amazing experiences."[28] Spielberg was presented to Queen Elizabeth when *E.T.* premiered in London; when he gave a special screening to President and Mrs. Reagan, he says that Nancy was crying toward the end of the film while the president "looked like a 10-year-old kid."[29] Once again, a Steven Spielberg movie had broken all box-office records, grossing $700 million before merchandising— another financial market into which Spielberg had recently entered. *E.T.* earned at least $1 billion in movie-related items, with Spielberg getting 10 percent of each item sold. He also had full approval of the products before they were put on the market. In 1985, Spielberg spoke out against videos, but when fans clamored for *E.T.*, he realized their profitability and relented in 1988. He received 50 percent of the video's profits, eventually making $70 million from video sales alone. The video was released again during the film's twentieth anniversary, this time with "Behind the Scenes" among the bonus features. The *Rolling Stone* wrote, "At 34, Steven Spielberg is in any conventional sense the most successful movie director in Hollywood, America, the Occident, the planet Earth, the solar system and the galaxy."[30] Nominated for nine Oscars, the movie won best music, best sound effects, and best special effects. Spielberg was again nominated for best director but lost to Richard Attenborough *(Gandhi)*, who said that he believed *E.T.* to be the more "exciting, wonderful, innovative piece of film."[31] The movie was extraordinary in other ways as well. One report is that an autistic child spoke his first words after seeing the movie. (True or not, it's a great tale.) Spielberg saw it as "a celebration of friendship and love and promoting understanding between races and cultures."[32] *Time* reporter Richard Corliss wrote, "A miracle movie and one that confirms Spielberg as a master storyteller of his medium . . . . A perfectly poised mixture of sweet comedy and ten-speed melodrama, of death and resurrection, of a friendship so pure and powerful it seems like an idealized love."[33] Spielberg was quite happy with the results of the movie *and* with the cleansing effect it had on his childhood memories. "I'm not into psychoanalysis, but *E.T.* is a film that was inside me for many years and could only come out after a lot of suburban psychodrama. . . . With the exception of *Close Encounters*, in all my movies before *E.T.*, I was giving out, giving off, things before I would bring them in. There were feelings I developed in my personal life . . . that I had no place to put."[34] Spielberg also discovered how much he loved working with children and realized that he wanted to be a father. From the very beginning, everything about the movie fell into place, which he saw as a sign that it was the right movie at the right time.

TWILIGHT ZONE THE MOVIE

Sadly, the huge success of *E.T.* was followed by tragedy during the filming of *Twilight Zone The Movie*, released in 1983. Four directors filmed four episodes, all but one being remakes of episodes from the original television series, *Twilight Zone* (CBS, 1959–1987). Spielberg directed the second segment, "Kick the Can," which tells the story of an old man who visits a retirement home and gives the residents back their youthful bodies. But it was while John Landis was directing his segment that a helicopter crashed into star Vic Morrow and two Asian child-actors, Renee Chen and My-ca Dinh Le, killing all three instantly. Morrow's daughters filed a lawsuit in 1982, alleging that drugs and alcohol were used on the set. Authors Stephen Farber and Marc Green write that in November 1983, the Morrow daughters received a settlement between $800,000 and $900,000. Other lawsuits were filed, including one by each set of the parents of the children who were killed. (Information about these settlements is unavailable.) On December 1, 1982, Spielberg signed a sworn statement to the National Transportation and Safety Board that he had never been on that set. The set's chauffeur, Carl Pittman, swore that Spielberg was not only on the set but had asked him for use of the car after the accident. He later recanted when he could not identify the director. Everyone else swore that Spielberg was never on the set, and he was cleared of any wrongdoing. John Landis was tried and acquitted for involuntary manslaughter. One of the jurors, Crispin Bernardo, said, "The fact that Landis was acquitted doesn't mean he's not guilty of anything. His acquittal does not mean lack of guilt, but insufficiency of proof."[35] Other jurors added that had the charge been violating child labor laws, the verdict would have been guilty. The movie was budgeted around $10 million, and it made approximately $6,614,000 its opening weekend. Eventually, it grossed around $29,500,000 in the United States. It was nominated for four different awards but no Oscars. The only time that Spielberg spoke publicly about the incident was in an interview with Dale Pollock of the *Los Angeles Times* on April 13, 1983. "This has been," he says, "the most interesting year of my film career. It has mixed the best, the success of *E.T.*, with the worst, the *Twilight Zone* tragedy. A mixture of ecstasy and grief. It has made me grow up a little more. The accident cast a pall on all 150 people who worked on this production. We are still just sick to the center of our souls."[36]

NOTES

1. Quoted in Chris Hodenfield, "*1941*: Bombs Away." *Rolling Stone*, January 24, 1980, reprinted in *Steven Spielberg Interviews*, Lester D. Friedman and Brent Notbohm, eds. (Jackson: University Press of Mississippi, 2000), 70.

2. Quoted in Frank Sanello, *Spielberg: The Man, The Movies, The Mythology* (Dallas: Taylor, 1996), 76.

3. Quoted in Hodenfield, 72.

4. Quoted in Sanello, 79.

5. Quoted in Sanello, 83.

6. Quoted in Susan Goldman Rubin, *Steven Spielberg: Crazy for Movies* (New York: Harry N. Abrams, 2001), 46.

7. Sanello, 90.

8. Quoted in Sanello, 97.

9. Quoted in Sanello, 98.

10. Quoted in Sanello, 94.

11. Quoted in Sanello, 96.

12. Roger Ebert, *The Great Movies II* (New York: Broadway Books, 2005), 344.

13. Quoted in Sanello, 92.

14. Sanello, 92.

15. Sanello, 99.

16. Richard Schickel, "Slam! Bang! A Movie Movie," *Time*, June 15, 1981, reprinted in *Steven Spielberg Interviews*, Lester D. Friedman and Brent Notbohm, eds. (Jackson: University Press of Mississippi, 2000).

17. Ibid.

18. Quoted in Sanello, 91.

19. Quoted in Sanello, 117–118.

20. Sanello, 118.

21. Quoted in Sanello, 118.

22. Quoted in Sanello, 119.

23. Sanello, 119.

24. Quoted in Sanello, 119–120.

25. Sanello, 120.

26. Linda Sunshine, ed., *E.T. the Extra-Terrestrial: From Concept to Classic*. The Illustrated Story of the Film and the Filmmakers Series (New York: Newmarket Press, 2002), 37.

27. Quoted in Sunshine, 40.

28. Quoted in Rubin, 53.

29. Ibid.

30. Quoted in Sanello, 103.

31. Quoted in Rubin, 53.

32. Quoted in Sunshine, 8.

33. Quoted in Sunshine, 168.

34. Quoted in Michael Sragow, "A Conversation with Steven Spielberg." *Rolling Stone*, July 22, 1982, reprinted in *Steven Spielberg Interviews*, Lester D. Friedman and Brent Notbohm, eds. (Jackson: University Press of Mississippi, 2000), 108, 109–110.

35. Quoted in Stephen Farber and Marc Green, *Outrageous Conduct: Art, Ego, and the Twilight Zone Case* (New York: Ivy, 1989), 322.

36. Quoted in Farber and Green, 133–134.

Chapter 4

REAL LIFE AND REEL LIFE, 1984–1991

HIS FIRST COMPANY: AMBLIN ENTERTAINMENT

In March 1982, Steven Spielberg almost bought a major studio with Francis Ford Coppola, Martin Scorsese, Brian DePalma, Michael Powell, and George Lucas. They bid up to $20 million for Pinewood Studios outside of London, but pulled out when the demanded price was raised to $30 million. One wonders what might have happened had these men formed a partnership. In 1984, Spielberg did form a production company with long-time friends, co-producers, and husband and wife team Frank Marshall and Kathleen Kennedy: Amblin Entertainment. With a logo showing Elliott and E.T. silhouetted against the moon, Amblin is located on the Universal Studio lot. It is in the southwestern style of architecture and features its own video arcade, full refreshment stand, kitchen with professional chef, screening and cutting rooms, a gym, and a wishing well with its own miniature shark. The walls of Spielberg's office are covered with movie posters and Norman Rockwell paintings. He discovered Rockwell when he was a Boy Scout and his troop kept a copy of the painter's "Spirit of America." He began collecting with the original of that painting and now owns at least 25. The Amblin headquarters is only two stories high because of Spielberg's fear of heights and elevators. The company has a television department, a merchandising division, an animation department, and a motion picture department. For the *New Yorker*, Stephen Schiff writes that Spielberg pretty much leaves the first two to others and enjoys the other two—as both a director and producer.

Spielberg says that he enjoys working with animation since "my imagination is becoming less and less affordable"[1] so he has "turned to animation as a way to free it up."[2] And with all of his success, he says that his children are most impressed with his cartoon productions, *Tiny Toons* and *Animaniacs*. In 1988, he and Lucas developed one of the most successful animation hits, *The Land Before Time*, and its nine straight-to-video sequels. Now that he has directed children in movies and become a father several times over—Max (Spielberg's), Jessica (Capshaw's), Sasha, Sawyer, Destry, Theo (adopted), and Mikaela (adopted)—Spielberg knows that even children's movies must be logical. "When my kids see movies, they'll buy anything if it sort of makes sense. But if they're confused, they get pulled out of the movie."[3] From *Continental Divide* to the hugely popular movie series, *Back to the Future*, Amblin Entertainment has produced some very successful and important movies, and there are more to come including *Indiana Jones 4* and *Jurassic Park IV*, both due out around 2008.

INDIANA JONES AND THE TEMPLE OF DOOM

When Steven Spielberg and George Lucas decided to make the first Indiana Jones movie in 1977, they also agreed to make two sequels if not three. Even so, Spielberg would later say that he made *Indiana Jones and the Last Crusade* (1989) to make up for *Indiana Jones and the Temple of Doom* (1984). Similarly, Lucas's second *Star Wars* movie, *The Empire Strikes Back*, is much darker than the original, and it was made around the same time, 1980–1983, as the second Indy movie. Both movies were darker because they reflected the lives of their creators at the time. George Lucas had been hit very hard by divorce and the ensuing huge financial settlement, and Spielberg—still shaken by the deaths on the *Twilight Zone* set—was also affected by the Lucas divorce because he had seen their marriage as a rare good one. When it failed, Spielberg said, "I lost my faith in marriage for a long time."[4]

In *Temple of Doom*, Indiana Jones winds up in a village in India where everyone is starving, crops will not grow, and all of the children have gone missing. The people think their travails are because of the theft of a sacred stone, so Indy sets out to retrieve the stone. He is accompanied by nightclub singer Willie Scott (Kate Capshaw) and Short Round (Ke Huy Quan). With a budget of $28 million, the cast and crew covered thousands of miles from California and Washington State to Sri Lanka and China. And Capshaw, after beating out 120 other actresses for the role, found herself spending five months on three continents in not-very-pleasant conditions. In one scene, she, Ford, and Ke Huy Quan had to walk through 20,000 insects. (Trivia: Insects are another Spielberg phobia.) They also had to endure 12-hour days in temperatures up to 130 degrees. In one scene, Capshaw was supposed to hold a 14-foot boa constrictor but Spielberg removed the scene for her. Spielberg was not happy at all with *Temple of Doom* and says that it lacks the personal touches and love that he normally puts into his movies. It was a dark movie with some horrific scenes—children working in mines and sacrificial pits, for examples. Younger audience members liked it but their parents were disappointed that George Lucas and Steven Spielberg would make such a film. Spielberg even had to fight to keep the movie from getting an "R" rating. The movie opened in the United States on Mary 23, 1984. It was nominated for two Academy Awards and won the Oscar for Best Visual Effects.

AMY IRVING

Spielberg may not have been pleased with *Temple of Doom*, but his relationship with Amy Irving was at a good place. The two first met when Irving auditioned for the role of Richard Dreyfuss's wife in *Close Encounters of the Third Kind*, but at 22 she was too young for the part. They met again at a dinner party, started dating, and soon began living together. They purposely made no movies together because Irving feared that she would be labeled as Steven Spielberg's girlfriend, and she wanted success on her own terms. They broke up in 1979. But in 1983, Spielberg traveled to India and ran into Irving at a movie site. They both seemed to have changed—she seemed less competitive and he seemed more open. They moved in together again. In September 1984, Spielberg told *Cosmopolitan* magazine, "I'm intolerably happy! I've been dedicated to films before. Now for the first time in my life, I'm committed to another person."[5] Their son, Max, was born on June 13, 1985, and the couple married on November 27, 1985. Spielberg was 37 and very ready to be a father. All the movies he had made with children had made him aware of how much he enjoyed them, but once Max was born, he no longer had the urge to have children in his movies. The couple built a home in the Hamptons, bought another in Trump Tower, and built Amblin Studios. In 1986, Irving went to Israel to make *Rumpelstiltskin*, and Spielberg went with her. (Trivia: She did the singing for Jessica Rabbit in the Spielberg-produced *Who Framed Roger Rabbit*.) Richard Dreyfuss says of Irving, "She's protective of her family and friends. I don't think she lets a lot of people get to know her. But if people perceive her as cold, it's not true. She's got a real soft heart. And she can hurt. She's very vulnerable. There's a side to Amy that is so giving and caring."[6] But the relationship just could not make it, and they divorced in 1989. Of Spielberg's estimated $1 billion, Irving received $100 million, a figure that still ranks among the highest marriage settlements in history. She and Spielberg agreed on joint custody of Max, and Spielberg stayed home with the child during his custodial periods. "By the time Max was one, I no longer had any choice. He took first place and nothing else would do."[7]

THE COLOR PURPLE

Happily settled down and glad to be finished with *Temple of Doom*, Spielberg wanted something different, and good friend and producer Kathleen Kennedy gave him a copy of Alice Walker's Pulitzer Prize–winning book, *The Color Purple*. Spielberg really wanted to direct it, but the story is about a black woman in rural Georgia in the first part of the twentieth century, and Spielberg was concerned that Walker might not have confidence in a white director bringing her characters to life. When Spielberg voiced his concern to Quincy Jones, the movie's producer, Jones responded, "You didn't have to go to outer space to make *E.T.*, did you?"[8] then added that the movie should be made by the director who loves it the most, and that was obviously Spielberg. Alice Walker agreed. She believed that any director who could make E.T. come so vividly to life was the right director for her book. At Spielberg's invitation and encouragement, Walker was always on the set to help with revisions. *The Color Purple* covers four decades in the life of Celie, who is raped and then has her baby taken from her. (Trivia: When filming the scene of Celie giving birth, Spielberg got the call that Max was being born, so he left the set. The voice of Celie's crying baby is actually Max Spielberg's voice.) She is separated from her only friend and confidant, her sister, and given in marriage to an older man who beats her. From a downtrodden girl who hides her smile, Celie grows into a strong independent woman who speaks her mind. As usual, Spielberg chose new or lesser-known actors for most of the parts. For the part of Celie, he chose stand-up comedienne, Whoopi Goldberg, who had not previously made a movie but has such an expressive face that the director cut 25 percent of her dialogue. He especially enjoyed directing her because she is a fellow movie buff who knew what he meant when he gave her a scene from another movie as his acting direction. Likewise, Oprah Winfrey was well known from her television talk show, but had never made a film. Spielberg hired her for her enthusiasm, her love of Walker's book, and her willingness to do anything to get the part. He and Quincy Jones had seen courage in her on TV. While it may not seem like it on first glance, Celie is Spielberg's "everyman." She is someone who wants to fulfill dreams, someone who seems ordinary yet accomplishes the extraordinary, and someone who overcomes victimization.

New York writer David Blum compared E.T. and Celie: "Both are outsiders in a strange, cruel world, struggling for freedom."[9]

Spielberg was still nervous about the project when production began in June 1985. For the first time he was making a film about adults—not aliens, children, or adventurers—and he was afraid he would not be able to reach the audience. "It's the risk of being judged—and accused of not having the sensibility to do character studies,"[10] he said in a 1985 interview. Spielberg did not use storyboards for the movie because he wanted each day to be new and an adventure. The movie's story was controversial, but its style was simple, one that used times of day and weather scenes to show the passing of time—portrayed exquisitely with Allen Daviau's cinematography. The genius of Quincy Jones and others created an equally superlative soundtrack. Spielberg took only the required Directors Guild minimum salary of $40,000, which he used to fund the movie's overages. At a cost of $15 million to produce, *The Color Purple* earned $142 million in just the United States and Canada, and it was nominated for 11 Academy Awards. The movie won no Oscars but it did win the Best Actress-Drama Award from the Golden Globes (for Goldberg) and Best Director's Award from the Directors' Guild of America (for Spielberg). Reviewers and other Hollywood moguls who had long enjoyed criticizing Spielberg for being good at making only action-adventure films were not about to quit criticizing and gave more attention to the fact that Spielberg was making a "serious" movie than to the quality of the movie itself.

AMAZING STORIES

Spielberg even tried television again when the medium lured him with an unbeatable deal: $1 million per half-hour episode, a guaranteed two-year run, full creative control, and no monitoring of his dallies. The series was *Amazing Stories*, and it ran from 1985 to 1987. NBC's head of programming, Brandon Tartikoff, expected something similar to *Alfred Hitchcock Presents* or *Twilight Zone*, eerie and a bit frightening, but Spielberg wanted a format that gave other filmmakers a chance to try television—and several big directors showed up: Martin Scorsese, Clint Eastwood, Paul Bartel, and Burt Reynolds. Spielberg directed two episodes—one about a World War II bombing mission, obviously made with his father in mind. In another episode, "Ghost Train," he directed Amy Irving, after their divorce and the only time he did so. Several other well-known actors appeared in the series: Drew Barrymore, Kevin Costner, Sid Caesar, Mark Hamill, Sam Waterston, Milton Berle, David Carradine, Stan Freberg, and Charlie Sheen. Spielberg expected the show to do very well, but the ratings proved disappointing, constantly sliding downward. Writer Pauline Kael said that Spielberg was now ripping off his own movies and that he was awfully young to be "paying homage to himself."[11] But Spielberg continued to produce successful movies and, in 1994, a successful television program, *ER*, which was still on the air as of 2006.

EMPIRE OF THE SUN

Steven Spielberg's fortieth birthday coincided with his next venture, *Empire of the Sun*, which he says is the "opposite of Peter Pan."[12] *Empire* is about "the death of innocence. . . . This was a boy who had grown up too quickly, who was becoming a flower long before the bud had ever come out of the topsoil."[13] Spielberg knew that many people had compared his life to a very long childhood, and he admitted it himself. Turning 40 and making more serious movies was, for him, a final step into adulthood. The *Los Angeles Times* even called *Empire of the Sun* Spielberg's "most mature and searing work to date."[14] Based on a fictionalized autobiography by J. G. Ballard, signs of Steven Spielberg run through the movie: his love of the World War II time period, his love of airplanes (even though he is afraid to fly), and a child's separation from his parents. The main character, Jim, lives in a wealthy colonial neighborhood in Shanghai where he is accustomed to servants. When the Japanese march into Shanghai on December 7, 1941, these families are forced into camps but Jim gets separated from his parents and spends the entire war in a different camp from them. Although a horrific idea, Ballard says that it was probably the best time in his life. He had no parental control and had to depend on his wits and personality to survive. And though he saw examples of Japanese brutality, he also got to know the Japanese as people and witness their dignity. His biggest adjustment was to life after the war. A person gets used to their security, whatever it is, says Ballard, and his security was the camp.

Spielberg had long wanted another movie such as *Duel* so he could tell a story almost exclusively through "visual metaphors and nonpretentious symbolism."[15] One of these is Jim witnessing the explosion over Hiroshima: the death of innocence—Jim's and the world's. *Empire of the Sun* was filmed in London and Shanghai—the first time that a U. S. film company was allowed to make a movie in the People's Republic of China. Allen Daviau was director of photography and Tom Stoppard wrote the screenplay albeit with Spielberg trademarks such as his love for Norman Rockwell, whose "Freedom from Fear" 1943 magazine cover goes with Jim wherever he goes. The actor who plays Jim, Christian Bale, was recommended to Spielberg by then-wife Amy Irving, who had worked with

Bale in *Anastasia: The Mystery of Anna* (1986). All Spielberg had to do to direct the 13-year-old was show him what to do and Bale copied him. When not filming, the two raced remote-controlled cars. Although making the movie was not enjoyable because of the dirty city and the movie's sad theme, Spielberg says the filmmaking process itself was the best he had ever experienced. The movie, released in 1987, received five Academy Award nominations, but it won none and was a flop at the box office, earning even less than *1941*, grossing only $66 million worldwide and making no money for the studio. But since Spielberg was assured a percentage of the gross, he still made money.

INDIANA JONES AND THE LAST CRUSADE

Even people as powerful as Steven Spielberg do not always get what they want. After spending five months developing *Rainman*, Spielberg had to hand it over, work and all, to Barry Levinson because he was obligated to George Lucas for the third Indiana Jones movie, *Indiana Jones and the Last Crusade*. (Trivia: He also wanted to direct *Big*, but his sister Anne had co-written the script and he did not want to steal any of her limelight.) Again, George Lucas and Spielberg collaborated. Lucas wanted a story about the Holy Grail and Spielberg wanted a father-son story and a subplot "that was almost stronger than the actual quest itself."[16] Harrison Ford liked the idea of the father character as a way to give more dimension to the Indy character, and they all liked the screenplay by Jeffrey Boam. Sean Connery was perfectly cast as Indy's father, and Spielberg says that it was hard not to laugh at the scenes with both men because their chemistry and timing were right on target. This third story begins with a flashback that shows Indy, played to perfection by River Phoenix, as a Boy Scout on a moving train filled with circus animals. The audience quickly learns why Indy hates snakes and how he learned to use a whip, but there were some ego problems. Ford was concerned with the energy and excitement in the Phoenix scenes and the amount of screen time they took. Phoenix had portrayed Ford's son in *Mosquito Coast* and had, writes Baxter, "almost stolen [the movie] from under his nose."[17] Lucas appeased his star by adding more action scenes. Connery, knowing that he was only 12 years older than Ford, was concerned that he appears "at least as potent as Ford."[18]

With a budget of $36 million, filming began on May 16, 1988, in a desert near Almeria, Spain. Other locations included Venice, Jordan, Austria, Germany, Colorado, New Mexico, Utah, and Texas. The "nasties" in this movie were rats—about 10,000 of them. Thinking that this would be the last of the Indiana Jones movies, Spielberg said, "I was going to make every effort to end the saga with a very unique and very thrilling finale."[19] But making this episode was so much fun that Spielberg finished filming with a "yes" to a fourth episode if the script is right. *Indiana Jones and the Last Crusade* opened May 24, 1989, and grossed $100 million before June 13. Spielberg, Lucas, and Ford had taken gross points instead of salaries, so their investment yielded very high returns. And while some critics enjoyed saying that Spielberg had returned to his old formula, Spielberg enjoyed knowing that there were theaters full of happy people. Author Baxter agrees. "After the violence and sadism of *Temple of Doom*, the tone was light, the humor effective, the characters likeable. . . . The old formula still worked."[20]

ALWAYS

With his love of old movies, it was only natural that Spielberg would want to recreate one of his favorites, *A Guy Named Joe* (1943) with Spencer Tracy. Actually, he did not want to remake the movie, but he could not find a story and script as good as the original. A project Spielberg had wanted to do for nine years, *Always* never quite came together even though it had a superb cast, another "real" people ensemble: Richard Dreyfuss, John Goodman, Holly Hunter, and Brad Johnson. Spielberg so enjoyed this cast that he gifted each with a Mazda Miata. While Spielberg may have been taking a chance with a love story, he was making a supernatural love story, which was right up his alley. Eight drafts of the script were written between 1980 and 1985, with four more written in 1985. The original story took place during World War II, and its main character was a pilot. Spielberg updated the movie to current times and made his main character a flying firefighter. He had discussed the movie with Dreyfuss during the filming of *Jaws*, and Dreyfuss desperately wanted the Tracy/leading role of Pete, the forest-fire pilot. Paul Newman and Robert Redford also wanted the role, but Dreyfuss was chosen for the usual reasons: He *is* the everyman with whom audiences can relate. Holly Hunter plays his girlfriend, Dorinda. The critics hated the movie, but it did fairly well at the box office when it opened in 1989. Costs came to $30 million and it grossed $77 million.

A SECOND CHANCE AT MARRIAGE

Spielberg met current wife, Kate Capshaw, when she auditioned for the part of nightclub singer Willie Scott in *Temple of Doom*. (Trivia: "Willie"

was Spielberg's dog's name.) Capshaw had taught educationally handicapped children for two years before going to New York City to look for
modeling and acting jobs. Not a fan of Spielberg's movies, she almost
decided not to audition for him, but the former soap-opera actress had just
moved to the area with her young daughter and needed the work. Spielberg says that Capshaw is a "natural" comedic actress—a "cross between
Lucille Ball and Ann Southern."[21] In his book, *Steven Spielberg: The Unauthorized Biography*, John Baxter writes that Capshaw fell in love with
Spielberg right away, and that Spielberg "was a pushover for the Texan
forthrightness of Capshaw."[22] Rumors abound about their relationship's
beginnings, but a year after Spielberg and Irving divorced, Spielberg and
Capshaw renewed their relationship. After a prenuptial agreement was
signed—a lesson learned from the Lucas divorce—the couple married on
October 12, 1991, in Spielberg's Long Island home then repeated their
vows at a civil service the next morning at Guild Hall. A third ceremony
was formal and traditional Jewish Orthodox and was followed by a recep-
tion filled with celebrities. A baby girl, Sasha, was born before their marriage and a son, Sawyer, followed soon after. Later they adopted a foster
child, Theo. (They later had Destry and adopted Mikaela.) Friends say
that Capshaw is "a nurturing, mothering type"[23] and that she and her
husband would rather spend time with friends and family than attend
Hollywood parties. Capshaw once asked her husband what had happened
to her career to which he replied, "You weren't supposed to have a career.
You were supposed to be with me."[24] And though Capshaw still makes the
occasional film, she says that she would rather be Spielberg's wife than
make a movie. Raised a Methodist, Capshaw converted to Judaism before
their marriage so their son would be born a Jew. She likes the religion
because of its emphasis on family. Spielberg had never been strong in his
faith until Capshaw made it a part of the family, but he has grown in it
ever since, and he is grateful to his wife for providing a warm and nurturing homelife.

NOTES

1. Quoted in "Steven Spielberg." Authors and Artists for Young Adults, vol.
24, Gale Research, 1998, reproduced in *Biography Resource Center* (Farmington
Hills, MI: Thomson Gale, 2005). www.galenet.galegroup.com/servlet/BioRC.

2. Ibid.

3. Quoted in Stephen Schiff, "Seriously Spielberg." *New Yorker*, March 21,
1994, reprinted in *Steven Spielberg Interviews*, Lester D. Friedman and Brent Notbohm, eds. (Jackson: University Press of Mississippi, 2000), 184.

4. Quoted in John Baxter, *Mythmaker: Life & Work of George Lucas* (New York: Avon, 1999), 343.

5. Quoted in Frank Sanello, *Spielberg: The Man, The Movies, The Mythology* (Dallas: Taylor, 1996), 151.

6. Quoted in Sanello, 190.

7. Quoted in Sanello, 192.

8. Quoted in Glenn Collins, "Spielberg films—*The Color Purple.*" *The New York Times*, December 15, 1985, reprinted in *Steven Spielberg Interviews*, Lester D. Friedman and Brent Notbohm, eds. (Jackson: University Press of Mississippi, 2000), 122–123.

9. Quoted in "Steven Spielberg," Authors and Artists for Young Adults, vol. 24.

10. Quoted in Collins, 120.

11. Quoted in Sanello, 172.

12. Quoted in Myra Forsberg, "Spielberg at 40: The Man and the Child." *The New York Times*, January 10, 1988, reprinted in *Steven Spielberg Interviews*, Lester D. Friedman and Brent Notbohm, eds. (Jackson: University Press of Mississippi, 2000), 127.

13. Ibid.

14. Quoted in Sanello, 180.

15. Quoted in Forsberg, 128.

16. Quoted in Marcus Hearn, *The Cinema of George Lucas* (New York: Harry N. Abrams, 2005), 159.

17. Baxter, 376.

18. Ibid.

19. Quoted in Sanello, 185.

20. Baxter, 377.

21. Quoted in Sanello, 142.

22. Baxter, 338–339.

23. Sanello, 195.

24. Quoted in Sanello, 196.

Chapter 5

FROM PETER PAN TO
COMPANY MAN, 1991–1994

In 1990, Steven Spielberg felt "artistically stalled."[1] When he tried to make more mature films, the critics flailed him and the audiences stayed away. When he signed with "the most powerful agent in Hollywood, Mike Ovitz,"[2] a studio executive said, "If anybody can finally get Spielberg off producing his umpteenth knockoff of *Jaws* and *E.T.* and directing grown-up movies, it's Ovitz at CAA [Creative Artists Agency]."[3] Spielberg had been upset that his people were passing on very good scripts such as *Dead Poets Society* and *Silence of the Lambs*. CAA was to assure him "first crack at the agency's 300-plus client list of writers and access to the agency's roster of A-list actors."[4]

HOOK

Their first collaboration was *Hook*, about a grown-up Peter Pan. Spielberg had wanted to make the movie in 1985, but the birth of his son convinced him that he "couldn't be Peter Pan anymore. I had to be his father."[5] But as his family increased, so did his interest in the fabled character, and when he read the Jim Hart script, he saw how much it related to today's busy lifestyle and lack of family time. He also liked the childlike wonderment mixed with "witty adult satire."[6] And what better movie to show Spielberg's love of flying? "To me, flying is synonymous with freedom and unlimited imagination,"[7] he says. Mike Ovitz likes to package movie deals, consolidating the agency's actors, directors, and writers, and *Hook* had been packaged with another director, but when Spielberg showed interest in the project, the other director was paid *not* to make the movie. Although it was rumored that Spielberg had talked of starring Michael Jackson in the leading role, it is Robin Williams who portrays the adult Peter Pan (aka greedy lawyer Peter Banning), who must return to Neverland to rescue his children from Captain Hook's clutches. Julia Roberts plays Tinkerbell and Dustin Hoffman plays Captain Hook. Such big names went against Spielberg's love of the "everyman" cast of unknowns. In fact, he is supposed to have said that he never wanted anyone who had been on the cover of *Rolling Stone*, and all three of these stars had been. Spielberg found himself with an entire group of egos to pacify. The major stars began clashing right away. Hoffman brought a script doctor to punch up his lines, while Williams was grossly insecure about playing to Hoffman. (Eventually, Spielberg, Hoffman, and Williams became good friends.) Julia Roberts was going through personal problems, some of which caused production to shut down for a week. Then there was her highly publicized cancelled wedding to Kiefer Sutherland followed by a weeklong trip to Ireland with her new boyfriend, Jason Patric. And then there was being late on the set; one time when Julia kept the cast and crew waiting she showed up saying, "I'm ready now." Spielberg's reply? "We're ready when *I* say we're ready, Julia."[8] When rumors flew that Spielberg was going to replace Roberts, the two held a joint press conference to squelch them. After the movie was completed, Spielberg told *60 Minutes* that he would never work with Roberts again. The actress was hurt and said that she had considered him a good friend and thought they had finished the production on good terms. There were other problems—such as making adults fly convincingly, controlling the large number of children in the cast, and controlling expenses—but Spielberg had learned that if he worried about costs while directing, he might compromise his creativity.

Most of the $60 million budget went to the elaborate sets. Studio executives were very pleased with the movie, and preview audiences gave it a 95 percent approval rating. The head of Tri-Star, Mike Medavoy, said the movie was "the pinnacle of his achievement. This is his real shot at the Oscar!"[9] Most critics, however, did not agree and called it "bloated" and "overproduced."[10] One critic, George Perry, wrote that it was "quite simply the best kids' film in many years."[11] The movie opened in the United States in December 1991. At a cost of approximately $70 million to produce, it recouped its cost and received five Academy Award nominations. CAA had worked out a very rich deal for Spielberg, Hoffman, and Williams: 40 percent of gross profits, with Hoffman and Williams taking nothing up front.

JURASSIC PARK

Steven Spielberg once asked a Harvard psychologist why so many children are fascinated with dinosaurs. The psychologist said it is because dinosaurs are "big, they're fierce . . . and they're dead."[12] The rights to Michael Crichton's book about dinosaurs, *Jurassic Park,* were on the bidding block, and Crichton chose Steven Spielberg, whom Crichton calls, "the most experienced and most successful director of these kinds of movies."[13] Spielberg saw the plot as a sequel to *Jaws* but on dry land. The movie can also be seen as a cross between a zoo and a theme park but with inhabitants that are dinosaurs that have been cloned from a fossil. Preproduction began in 1990 and took two years. Spielberg storyboarded and had artists make sketches for the more complicated scenes. Special effects genius Stan Winston was in charge of building the life-size creatures, some of which had "stand-ins" for various scenes. The 20-foot Tyrannosaurus Rex weighed 13,000 pounds and was operated by remote control. The full-sized velociraptors were either a full-sized puppet or a suit worn by an actor. In addition, Spielberg went to George Lucas's Industrial Light and Magic (ILM), where computer-generated images (CGI) were so realistic that some of the models were not used at all. According to Lucas biographer Marcus Hearn, Lucas said, "when we put [the dinosaurs] [sic] on the screen everyone had tears in their eyes. It was like one of those moments in history, like the invention of the light bulb or the first telephone call."[14] The unofficial word is that using CGI saved the studio $10 million. To obtain such realism, Spielberg had sent the computer masters to mime classes to become more aware of their body movements. They were filmed as each one ran the way a specific dinosaur would have done and then watched the film to see how their weight shifted, etc. As Spielberg once said, an audience will believe fantasies if they are made convincingly and seriously. The robots with CGI "mates" were electronically encoded so that each moved together. Real sounds were collected and then combined and changed to give each creature its proper voice. The final products, says Spielberg, "exceeded my expectations. . . . It was everything I wanted it to be—no less and a lot more."[15]

Using computer graphics means that the actors have to act "to" a blue screen and cannot see the results until the movie is put together. When actress Ariana Richards (Lex Murphy) saw the movie, she says that the stampede scene was "breathtaking"[16] and that some scenes scared her even though she had been part of them. The actors who co-starred with the dinosaurs were Sir Richard Attenborough, Sam Neill, Laura Dern, and Jeff Goldblum. All are highly respected but without the superstar status and accompanying egos that Spielberg tries to avoid. Filming began in Kauai, Hawaii, on August 24, 1992, and ended with a hurricane. Producer Kathleen Kennedy says, "If you're going to be stranded with anyone, be stranded with a movie crew. We had generators for lights and plenty of food and water."[17] Spielberg was so good at entertaining the children that they barely realized what was going on. Even with the hurricane, the movie came in under budget and a few days early. *Jurassic Park* was released on June 10, 1993, and soon became the biggest box-office draw up to that time, and the winner of three Oscars.

SPEAKING OF MONEY

Jurassic Park's total earnings eventually went up to more than $900 million and Spielberg's final receipts were $294 million. According to *Forbes* magazine, this was "the most ever made by 'a single individual from a movie or other form of entertainment.'"[18] Along with Oprah Winfrey, Spielberg topped *Forbes* list of billionaire entertainers in 2005. In 1994, *Forbes* magazine called him "the first billionaire director."[19] In 2006, the magazine listed his worth at $2.8 billion. In his 1999 interview with Spielberg, Stephen J. Dubner writes that Spielberg is "very good at making money. While he is considered to be courtly in creative matters, his reputation as a negotiator is far less benign."[20] Spielberg knows that his clout in Hollywood prevents people from telling him "no," so he knows that *he* has to be responsible in his business dealings. And while he has not taken a salary in many years, he has "the sweetest of sweetheart deals."[21] For *Jurassic Park*, Universal received 50 percent of gross earnings. Spielberg received 17.5 percent of that, *and* 50 percent of Universal's profits plus reimbursement for production, advertising, and distribution costs. He then gets 100 percent of Amblin's profits, since he is the sole owner, then gets 50 percent of video sales, 50 percent of TV/cable fees, and 50 percent of royalties on the movie's merchandise sales. And, writes Dubner, "The movies are only the engine of Spielberg's entertainment machine. There are the television shows and cartoons he has produced, a joint venture to build futuristic video arcades and . . . a Universal Studios theme park in Orlando for which he is a creative consulant. All told, he is worth an estimated $2 billion, which has led to many whispers that his taste for money exceeds his taste for art."[22] And he constantly finds new venues in which to get involved. His curiosity seems insatiable.

SCHINDLER'S LIST

After his next movie, no one could ever accuse Steven Spielberg of making only action-adventure films. "Everything I have done up 'till now has really been in preparation for *Schindler*. I had to grow into that."[23] Of course, there were detractors who said he was making the movie only to win an Oscar, but it is unlikely that he would have put himself through such an emotional roller coaster for an award. "Every day," says Spielberg, "shooting *Schindler's List* was like waking up and going to hell." Yet, at the time, he also said, "I feel more connected with the material than I've ever felt before."[24]

Oskar Schindler was an industrialist and member of the Czechoslovakian Nazi Party during World War II who became wealthy during the war. He is celebrated because he used that wealth to rescue Jews from concentration camps by giving them jobs in his factory. By war's end, he had saved more than a thousand people. In later years he earned the title of Righteous Gentile from the Yad Vashem in Israel. (Yad Vashem is a worldwide organization that researches the Holocaust to keep alive the memories of the six million who died.) Thomas Keneally wrote the book, *Schindler's List*, after a chance meeting with one of Schindler's survivors, Poldek Pfefferberg (who changed his name to Leopold Page), who told Keneally his story. When Keneally's book came out in 1982, Spielberg was drawn to it immediately, but did not feel "emotionally ready to take a chance with the Holocaust."[25] But he certainly received encouragement to make it. Producer Sid Sheinberg bought the rights in 1982 and told Spielberg that this was a movie that he must make. When Leopold Page met Spielberg in 1983, he asked him when he was going to make the movie. Even Spielberg's mother asked him the same question, and between 1982 and 1993 the film was never far from his thoughts. As he mulled over ways to make the best possible movie, he remembered the taunts and cruel treatment he had received in high school just because of his faith. One sign that the time was right to make the movie was when he learned that 60 percent of recent high school graduates had never heard of the Holocaust. Another sign was when his wife converted to Judaism and made the religion a regular part of the family's practices. Everything was coming together to make Spielberg not only ready to make the film, but eager to embrace his heritage. "I was so ashamed of being a Jew," he says, "and now I'm filled with pride. I don't even know when that transition happened."[26]

The decision made, Spielberg set out to use his talents to make the movie he knew *Schindler's List* should be. His partnership with composer John Williams, which started with *Sugarland Express*, continued. When Williams saw the first cuts of the movie he told Spielberg that he needed a better composer. Spielberg's reaction? "I know," he told Williams, "but they're all dead."[27] Spielberg wanted a documentary feel but had a hard time convincing the producers that he should film in black and white with small snippets of color. "Every time I see anything in color about World

War II, it looks too glamorized, too antiseptic. I think black and white is almost the synonymous form for World War II and the Holocaust."[28] Black and white, he says, is "completely unforgiving. Black and white is about texture; it's not about tone. . . . black-and-white details every single wall, all the bricks, all the chipped plaster on the facades of these ghetto dwellings."[29] Universal Studios Chairman Tom Pollock saw video sales as the only way the movie would make a profit, so he begged Spielberg to film the movie in color. Spielberg agreed with Pollack that the movie would likely fail at the box office. How could a movie about the Holocaust be entertaining? Even worse to Spielberg—if the movie *were* entertaining, he would feel that he had failed. "It was important to me not to set out to please. Because I always had."[30] But both men were wrong in their expectations. In the March 21, 1994, issue of the *New Yorker,* Stephen Schiff writes, "Of course, the almost unmentionable secret of *Schindler's List* is that it does entertain; that part of its greatness comes from the fact that it moves swiftly and energetically, that it has storytelling confidence and flair. . . ."[31] Schiff also notes that the movie is really not so different from Spielberg's other work, because Schindler is the "everyman" character that Spielberg likes to use. Although Schindler is now seen as a hero, he was a very common and sometimes immoral man. Because of characters such as Schindler, writes Schiff, Spielberg "made it O.K. not to be remarkable by telling us that we already were."[32]

Spielberg instructed his director of photography, Janusz Kaminski, to use a handheld camera for most of the movie. He wanted no modern equipment used—no cranes, dollies, or zoom lenses. He wanted the movie to be timeless so future audiences would see a World War II movie, not a World War II movie made in 1993. They shot the film in actual locations in Krakow, Poland: the Jewish Ghetto, Auschwitz, and even Schindler's real factory and apartment. Because the World Jewish Congress refuses filming inside Auschwitz, Spielberg built an exact replica right outside the real thing. During preproduction, the director met Branko Lustig, a Croatian filmmaker and Holocaust survivor, and made him one of the movie's co-producers. When filming began on March 1, 1993, producer Jerry Molen said he believed that a "divine hand"[33] had been placed on Spielberg's shoulder, because when Spielberg needed snow, it snowed, and when he wanted it to stop, it stopped. The movie, budgeted at $22 million, had 126 speaking parts, approximately 30,000 extras, more than 210 crewmembers, and 148 sets in 35 locations. "Like running an army,"[34] says Spielberg's spokesperson, Martin Levy. Before shooting began, everyone met at Auschwitz for a memorial service. "There is an almost consecrated gravity to this set,"[35] writes John H. Richardson in his January 1994 *Premier* article. "It is a haunted killing field, and you feel it," says Spielberg.

"Everybody was extremely edgy the couple of days we shot there."[36] He and a technician had a particularly hard time filming the scene in which German guards are choosing which female prisoners—stripped naked and obviously embarrassed and frightened—will live and which will die. The scene took three days to film. "There was no break in the tension," says Spielberg. "Nobody felt there was any room for levity. I didn't expect so much sadness every day." Ben Kingsley says, "The ghosts were on the set every day in their millions."[37] The extras reported to wardrobe at five o'clock every morning, and the costumers made sure that the same people wore the same costume every day. Translators were needed to give directions to the non-English speakers, of which there were many, yet there were not enough Polish Jews to fill the parts because there were not enough left due to the Holocaust. As usual, Spielberg chose actors who were not widely known at the time. For the main character, Spielberg wanted someone very close in demeanor to the real man. "Oskar Schindler is the most romantic character I've ever worked with," said Spielberg. "He romances the entire city of Krakow, he romances the Nazis, he romances the politicians, the police chiefs, the women. He was a grand seducer."[38] He chose Liam Neeson. Schindler hires Itzhak Stern (Ben Kingsley) to keep his business records. The antagonist is the camp's commandant, Amon Goeth (Ralph Fiennes), a charming but deranged killer. Spielberg sees the movie as being a fight between Stern and Goeth—good and evil—to win Schindler's soul.

Israeli actress Adi Nitzan tells of the day she went to eat lunch in the commissary and started to sit with men in Nazi uniforms, but the contrast of her rags to their dignified uniforms made her want to cry. Spielberg says that he had the same reaction when he was directing the uniform-clad actors. "Just think," Spielberg said, "I'm standing right here where 50 years ago people were loaded on trucks. If it were not for a different time. . . "[39] When Liam Neeson complained about the freezing weather, Lustig showed him the tattoo on his arm and reminded him that he and millions of others had lived through such weather with barely enough food, clothes, and shelter. But no matter the costume, all cast and crew were on the same side and participated in a seder. All the men wore yarmulkes and read from the seder text as Israelis helped the gentiles understand the service. Says Spielberg, "Race and culture were just left behind."[40] He did, however, worry about making a hero out of a Nazi (Schindler) and recalled when the movie *Das Boot* was released and the resulting uproar over making German sailors (even non-Nazis) heroes. Spielberg decided that if such a furor arose with *Schindler's List* he would hold a press conference with some of the survivors. As it happened, the end of the movie did the trick. Joyous color fills the screen as the happy faces of the survivors' and/or their descendents begin descending down a hill. Each person is accompanied by the actor who portrays him or her in the movie, and each person places a rock on Oskar Schindler's grave. When Schindler died in 1974, his will revealed that he wanted to be buried in the Catholic Cemetery on Mt. Zion in Jerusalem, and that is where he is. Before the epilogue, the last scenes in the movie show the survivors using a man's gold filling to make Schindler a ring with the inscription, "You save one life, you save the world."[41] (In real life, the survivors also supported Schindler financially because his business ventures failed.) At the end of filming the movie, the remaining survivors made Steven Spielberg an exact replica of the ring with the same inscription. He later made replicas for Sid Sheinberg and Lew Wasserman at Universal.

Mondays through Fridays Spielberg worked on *Schindler,* and on weekends he continued editing *Jurassic Park.* Eventually, the race to get *Jurassic Park* to the theaters forced him to give it even more time, so he had it "fed" to a theater in Krakow. He now filmed *Schindler* in the daytime, spent evenings with his family, and then edited *Jurassic Park* at night. Spielberg rarely misses having dinner with his family and reading bedtime stories to his children, and he had brought his entire family with him—from his wife and children to his parents, his ill stepfather's entire medical team, and the family rabbi. He and Capshaw wanted the children to witness the history. He arranged a private screening for his mother and stepfather but could not watch the movie with them. His mother cried throughout the viewing and says she knew her son wanted her impression but she couldn't speak. "I was totally mute," she says. "I thought I would never speak again."[42] She was especially affected by the scene when the mothers are crying and running after their children as the children sing, "Oyfn Pripetchik," a Jewish alphabet song that Spielberg's grandmother used to sing to him. The irony is that the title actually means, "On the Wooden Stove."[43] His sister, Anne, saw the movie at the Simon Wiesenthal Center/Museum of Tolerance in Los Angeles and says that people were not just crying, they were sobbing and walking to their cars in silence. Sister Nancy says that seeing the movie was one of her proudest moments. In March 1994, *Schindler's List* was recognized at the Academy Awards with seven awards, including Best Picture and Best Director. In his thank-you address, Spielberg remembered the six million people who died in the Holocaust. The movie grossed $96 million in the United States and $321 million worldwide, the highest grossing black-and-white movie in history. Spielberg's salary had been only the mandatory minimum stipulated by the Directors Guild Union.

THE SCHINDLER/SPIELBERG LEGACY

With his percentage profits, Spielberg founded the Shoah Foundation, whose founding advisory committee includes the movie's producers, Jerry Molen and Branko Lustig. ("Shoah" is Hebrew for "Holocaust.") So many survivors wanted to tell Spielberg their personal stories that he realized they needed a place to do so, and a place where their stories would be saved forever. The foundation records firsthand accounts and prepares them so that anyone anywhere can call them up and learn about history from someone who witnessed it. He knows the importance of hearing the real voices and seeing the real faces as they speak. And Spielberg wants these accounts from all survivors, "all those people that the Nazis considered 'subhuman': Jews, Gypsies, Jehovah's Witnesses, homosexuals, and others."[44] Thousands of volunteers are trained and then sent to all corners of the globe to get these stories. They usually begin the interview by asking for descriptions of the person's life before the war. This makes the person comfortable sharing personal information with a stranger before they describe their wartime experiences. The camera films the interview in an unobtrusive manner. Each survivor receives a copy of his or her filmed interview. The original is put in computer format, catalogued, and then stored in an underground vault. The information is cross-indexed to aid victims locate lost friends and family members. Spielberg's dream and dedication is "to take as many testimonies as is humanly possible and make their stories available for no fee for those who want it."[45] As of September 2005, almost 52,000 testimonies have been collected in 56 countries and 32 languages. An interesting aspect of the foundation, too, is that Spielberg's father, Arnold Spielberg, is a consultant on the projects.

Spielberg has also produced a CD-Rom with the stories of four survivors, which he gives to teachers, and the Shoah Foundation produced three documentaries, one of which, *Last Days*, won an Oscar in 1998. In 2006, Spielberg produced *Spell Your Name*, in which survivors describe the World War II Babi Yar massacre in the Ukraine.

DREAMWORKS (SKG)

On October 12, 1994, Steven Spielberg took another large step when he teamed with Jeffrey Katzenberg and David Geffen to form their own film, television, music, and interactive software company. A former president of Disney, Katzenberg had had successes with *The Little Mermaid, Beauty and the Beast,* and *The Lion King*. Geffen was a music agent who founded two record companies, Asylum (1971) and Geffen (1980), and the Geffen Film Company, which produced the movies *Beetlejuice* and *Interview with the Vampire*. Spielberg and Katzenberg teamed up in 1988 to produce *Who Framed Roger Rabbit* and became partners in Dive! a family-oriented submarine-shaped restaurant in Los Angeles. (Dive! went out of business in January 1999.) It was originally Katzenberg's idea to form the movie company. Spielberg did not want to leave MCA/Universal because its president, Sidney Sheinberg, had given him his first directing job and become the young director's mentor and friend; but when Spielberg learned that Sheinberg was leaving MCA, he talked to the older man about his plans. Sheinberg asked Spielberg why he wanted his own company, and Spielberg replied, "It benefits me because the idea of building something from the ground up, where I could actually be a co-owner, where I don't rent, I don't lease, I don't option but actually own; that appeals to me."[46] Sheinberg gave his blessing. Now past the first hurdle, Spielberg and Katzenberg could give into their dreams of creating "a studio designed from the perspective of filmmakers."[47] The two men thought of themselves as trailblazers such as those who had formed United Artists in 1919: Douglas Fairbanks, Charlie Chaplin, Mary Pickford, and D. W. Griffith.

The second hurdle was Mrs. Steven Spielberg: Kate Capshaw. Katzenberg was a known workaholic, so Capshaw put down ground rules. Her husband is available to work *only* after he takes the kids to school in the morning; and he *must* be home by six on weekdays. He must be home all day every weekend. This is also what Spielberg wants, because his family is so important to him. He is often described as a family man who might drive a Porsche, but who drives that Porsche into a 7-Eleven to buy a Slurpie. Finally, Katzenberg had to convince Spielberg that they needed David Geffen: "an executive who was schooled in the music business but who was also a financial wizard with outstanding creative instincts."[48] In Tom King's biography of David Geffen, he writes that Steven Spielberg and David Geffen had a history of "butting heads"[49] because Spielberg had a strong moral conscience while Geffen "had his own ideas of what was right and what was wrong."[50] But King also writes that Geffen may be the only person who can speak to Steven Spielberg as an equal, which helped especially when dealing with finances. Geffen had sold Geffen Records in 1990 and was enjoying a quiet life, but after some indecision, he decided to join the other two moguls. When the press nicknamed them "The Dream Team," Spielberg suggested that their official company name be DreamWorks SKG (SKG standing for each man's last initial). (Trivia: DreamWorks insured Spielberg's life for $1.2 billion.) The logo is a little boy sitting on the moon with a fishing pool—an obvious

Spielberg design. Spielberg's spokesperson, Marvin Levy, says the boy is "trolling for ideas."[51]

Author Tom King writes that business for the three men did not change noticeably. Spielberg continued to run Amblin, Geffen was involved with a record label, and Katzenberg was running a feature/animation department. In addition, Spielberg had agreed from the beginning that he would still direct movies for other studios. The studio's first movie, *Amistad* (1997) (see chapter 6), was not a financial success. When Spielberg wanted to direct *Saving Private Ryan* (see chapter 6), Geffen went to the head of parent company Paramount (who owned the script) and told them that Spielberg would not direct unless DreamWorks got 50 percent of the profits and 50 percent of the distribution rights. The other selling point was that DreamWorks would split their profits with Paramount on the disaster movie *Deep Impact* (1998), which turned out to be the second highest grossing film in DreamWorks's first five years. When *Saving Private Ryan* turned out to be a huge hit, investor/entrepreneur Paul Allen purchased more shares of DreamWorks stock and became the company's largest stockholder with 24 percent. The SKG men held 22 percent. Spielberg won the Best Director Oscar for *Saving Private Ryan*, but the movie lost out to *Shakespeare in Love* for best movie. Because of the studio losing the big award, the DreamWorks/Paramount after-Oscar party was "more like a wake than a party,"[52] writes King.

One of Spielberg's dreams for the new film company was to build a studio at a site known as Playa Vista near the Los Angeles International Airport. In April 1999, DreamWorks signed on to buy the 47 acres for $20 million, but the film company could not get conventional bank financing to back the construction. The three owners plus entrepreneur Paul Allen could have raised the money easily with personal funds, but they finally decided that they did not want to invest so much and backed out. Dream-Works would not have its large new building. In fact, by mid-2005, the company was having problems, and talk of selling became headline news. In their article for *Time* magazine, Daniel Kadlec and Jeffrey Ressner write that none of the owners are professional CEOs and that they have made some mistakes. Stephen Dubner reports that Spielberg told him that "expectations were too high to begin with."[53] In December 2005, Paramount Pictures announced that it was buying DreamWorks for $1.6 billion in cash and debt. (The purchase did not include DreamWorks Animation SKG Inc.) Then, in March 2006, Paramount announced that it was selling the films of DreamWorks to billionaire George Soros for $900 million. On March 12, 2006, a *New York Times* article describes all of the ins and outs of the financial dealings and speculates as to whether or not Paramount made a good deal. Among other suggestions is, "It may be more about images than numbers. Paramount will have the cachet of being associated with Mr. Spielberg . . ."[54] Not only does the director still have Amblin Entertainment and a "long-term deal with NBC Universal,"[55] but he will continue to direct and produce some movies for DreamWorks.

NOTES

1. Frank Sanello, *Spielberg: The Man, The Movies, The Mythology* (Dallas: Taylor, 1996), 205.

2. Sanello, 206.

3. Quoted in Sanello, 206.

4. Sanello, 206.

5. Quoted in Ana Maria Bahiana, "*Hook,*" Cinema Papers, March–April 1992, reprinted in *Steven Spielberg Interviews*, Lester D. Friedman and Brent Notbohm, eds. (Jackson: University Press of Mississippi, 2000), 153.

6. Sanello, 208.

7. Quoted in Bahiana, 153.

8. Quoted in Sanello, 211.

9. Quoted in Sanello, 213.

10. Ibid.

11. Ibid.

12. Quoted in Susan Goldman Rubin, *Steven Spielberg: Crazy for Movies* (New York: Harry N. Abrams, 2001), 60.

13. Ibid.

14. Quoted in Marcus Hearn, *The Cinema of George Lucas* (New York: Harry N. Abrams, 2005), 174.

15. Quoted in *The Making of Jurassic Park*, directed by Steven Spielberg. *Jurassic Park* Collector's Edition, DVD. Universal City, CA: Universal, 2000.

16. Quoted in Rubin, 66.

17. Quoted in Rubin, 65.

18. Quoted in Sanello, 218.

19. Sanello, 218.

20. Stephen J. Dubner, "Inside the Dream Factory," *Guardian Unlimited*, March 21, 1999. www.guardian.co.uk.

21. Ibid.

22. Ibid.

23. Quoted in Rubin, 67.

24. Quoted in Sanello, 227.

25. Quoted in Rubin, 68.

26. Quoted in John H. Richardson, "Steven's Choice." *Premiere*, January 1994, reprinted in *Steven Spielberg Interviews*, Lester D. Friedman and Brent Notbohm, eds. (Jackson: University Press of Mississippi, 2000), 165.

27. Quoted in Rubin, 73.

28. Quoted in Bahiana, 156.

29. Quoted in Richardson, 164.

30. Quoted in Stephen Schiff, "Seriously Spielberg." *New Yorker,* March 21, 1994, reprinted in *Steven Spielberg Interviews,* Lester D. Friedman and Brent Notbohm, eds. (Jackson: University Press of Mississippi, 2000), 176.

31. Schiff, 176.

32. Schiff, 180.

33. Quoted in Rubin, 70.

34. Ibid.

35. Richardson, 158.

36. Quoted in Richardson, 159.

37. Quoted in Sanello, 228.

38. Quoted in Richardson, 161.

39. Quoted in Rubin, 74.

40. Quoted in Sanello, 228.

41. Ibid.

42. Quoted in Rubin, 73.

43. Hebrewsongs, "Oyfn Pripetchik," www.hebrewsongs.com, accessed May 23, 2006.

44. Quoted in Rubin, 76.

45. Quoted in Rubin, 76–77.

46. Quoted in Tom King, *The Operator: David Geffen Builds, Buys, and Sells the New Hollywood* (New York: Random House, 2000), 527.

47. King, 528.

48. King, 521.

49. King, 522.

50. Ibid.

51. Quoted in Rubin, 78.

52. King, 583.

53. Dubner.

54. Andrew Ross Sorkin, "A Happy Ending for Some, a Comedy of Errors for Others," *The New York Times,* March 12, 2006. www.nytimes.com.

55. Walter Scott, "Walter Scott's Personality Parade," *Parade Magazine* in *Seattle Times,* September 11, 2005, 2.

Jaws (1975) made Steven Spielberg a major director and set the standard for future adventure movies. Shown on the set from left: Robert Shaw ("Quint"), Roy Scheider ("Police Chief Martin Brody"), Steven Spielberg, and Richard Dreyfuss ("Matt Hooper"). *Source*: Universal Pictures/Photofest.

E.T. the Extra-Terrestrial (1982) is still Steven Spielberg's favorite movie and the one that best represents his personal feelings. Drew Barrymore auditioned for *Poltergeist* and is Spielberg's goddaughter. Shown on the set from left: Steven Spielberg, and Drew Barrymore ("Gertie"). *Source*: Universal Pictures/Photofest.

Indiana Jones and the Temple of Doom (1984) is the second in the Indiana Jones trilogy. It is also the movie that brought Spielberg and Capshaw together. Shown off the set from left: Kate Capshaw ("Wilhelmina 'Willie' Scott"), Steven Spielberg, George Lucas, and Harrison Ford ("Indiana Jones"). *Source:* Paramount Pictures/Photofest.

Schindler's List (1993) is probably the most respected of Spielberg's movies. It is also the one that brought the director close to his Jewish roots, and the one that won him his first Best Director Academy Award. Shown on the set from left: Steven Spielberg and Liam Neeson ("Oskar Schindler"). *Source*: Universal Pictures/Photofest.

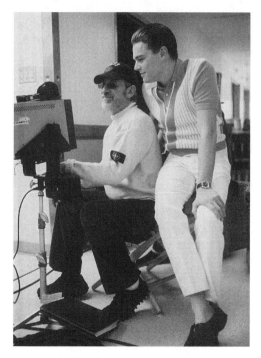

Catch Me If You Can (2002) is based on the true story of Frank Abagnale, Jr. who successfully passed himself off as numerous professional people. Shown off set from left: Steven Spielberg and Leonardo DiCaprio ("Frank Abagnale, Jr."). Tom Hanks also starred in the film. *Source*: DreamWorks/Photofest.

The Terminal (2004) is another Spielberg/Hanks collaboration. Hanks plays Viktor Navorski who makes the best of a bad situation when he is forced to live in the airport. Shown on set from left: Steven Spielberg and Catherine Zeta-Jones ("Amelia Warren"). *Source*: Dreamworks/Photofest.

Chapter 6

INTO THE NEW MILLENNIUM, 1994–2001

TAKING A BREAK FROM DIRECTING

With *Schindler's List*, Steven Spielberg achieved the serious respect previously denied him. But it was such an emotional project that he was tired and needed a break—but a break to Steven Spielberg does not mean a vacation. As one of the creative consultants to Islands of Adventure, Spielberg helped create Universal Orlando's main attraction. Based on *Jurassic Park*, the site has a river ride that drops you 80 feet beneath the open jaws of a Tyrannosaurus Rex. There are shady spots complete with caves and water cannons and a Discovery Center where you can watch the hatching of velociraptor eggs. There will also be *War of the Worlds* destruction by the 747 Jetliner. In April 2006, it was announced that there was to be a "Jurassic Park Institute Tour," an educational exhibit traveling through Asia. Spielberg is also producing movies and television programs for his studio, Amblin.

THE LOST WORLD JURASSIC PARK

When he felt like directing again, he returned to something familiar and fun: *The Lost World Jurassic Park*. Spielberg was not a big fan of sequels, but producer Kathleen Kennedy encouraged him to make them after audiences assumed that he had made the inferior sequels to *Jaws*. "There's a proprietary creative interest to protect and ensure the quality," she says.[1] Spielberg decided that if each sequel is a new story that can stand on its own with only the characters repeated, then he would make them, but he knows that his audiences are savvy and expect more in each sequel. Before *Jurassic Park*, they wondered if he could make dinosaurs. Now they knew he could make them, but what else could he do with them? (There will never be a sequel to *E.T.* Spielberg says, "I didn't want to do anything that would blemish its memory with a sequel that would not be—could not possibly be—its superior."[2]) One fan who really wanted a *Jurassic Park* sequel was an elementary school student who requested that a stegosaurus be added to the second movie. But, the child wrote, "Whatever you do, please don't have a long, boring part at the beginning that has nothing to do with the island."[3] Spielberg did not want long boring scenes at the beginning either, but he had to explain why intelligent human beings would return to such a dangerous place, which is actually one of the reasons that he wanted to make the movie: the idea of dinosaurs living in the wild. Spielberg sees *Jurassic Park* as the "failure of technology and the success of nature," and *The Lost World* as the "failure of people to find restraints within themselves and the failure of morality to protect these animals."[4] The plot of the *The Lost World Jurassic Park*: John Hammond (Richard Attenborough) tells Ian Malcolm (Jeff Goldblum) that the dinosaurs had been bred on a different island than the one with the park and that the remaining animals have thrived and multiplied. He wants Malcolm to research them, but when Malcolm and his group arrive, they find Hammond's nephew (Arliss Howard) making plans to take the animals to a dinosaur park in San Diego.

Spielberg set Michael Crichton up to writing the sequel and then began working with scriptwriter David Koepp. This time Spielberg used moving three-dimensional (3D) storyboards so that he could see if some of his ideas could really be done. He definitely wanted the creatures to be even better than in *Jurassic Park*, which meant they had to move more smoothly and be authentic enough to convince the paleontologist who helped create them from research to drawing to 3D sculptures to full size. Computer graphics and puppets were both used, with the former used for distance/action shots and the latter for close-ups. Real animals were videotaped and studied to assure even more reality to the movement of the creatures. By the time *The Lost World Jurassic Park* was made, the price of computer graphics was going down and the price of the robotic puppets was going up. Inner parts of the robots can be saved and used again, but the rubber skin cannot. Audiences become jaded very quickly, and, says Spielberg, the magic of movies is making the audience forget it is watching magic. The movie was filmed in Kauai, Hawaii, and Eureka, California, with a catholic girls' school in Pasadena used for Hammond's office. With 35–45 set-ups per day, it was fast moviemaking. Since Spielberg always knows what he wants and is always prepared, he films one scene while the next set is going up, so sets are always ready. Since the actors had to play to blue screens, Spielberg had dinosaur heads stuck onto sticks that were carried by crewmembers so the heads were at the correct height of the real creature. This enabled the actor to look in the correct direction and at the correct height. A field of real grass was even grown to make a scene with running raptors appear more realistic.

The movie's cost was estimated at $73 million, and its May 1997 opening weekend's U.S. box office was $92,729,064. It was nominated for the Academy Award for Best Visual Effects, and most reviewers agree that the movie is "a beautifully crafted series of nightmarish set pieces with no other goal in mind than to scare and delight the audience."[5]

AMISTAD

Spielberg's next project was another serious story based on another true event: the 1839 mutiny onboard the Spanish slave ship *Amistad*. As the ship was going from Havana to another port in Cuba, the slaves killed everyone but the two men who purchased them, saved only on the promise that they will take the Africans back home. Instead, they took the slaves to the United States and handed them over to a U.S. Navy ship near Connecticut. Laws regarding slavery were complicated and changed many times. In 1839, the international slave trade had been outlawed, but slavery was still very much in effect. Those who were already slaves or were the children of slaves were returned to their masters if they escaped. The *Amistad* slaves were put on trial. Their defense was that they were never slaves but were kidnapping victims, but if the state proved that the *Amistad* slaves were children of slaves, then they were not kidnapping victims but murderers. David Franzoni wrote the story from Cinque's point of view. He did not want it to be just an antislavery story, especially since Cinque was never a slave. Steve Zaillian, the writer of *Schindler's List*, was brought in for rewrites because Spielberg likes his realistic dialogue. Spielberg used little camera movement, so the viewer feels transported to the nineteenth century. In the book *Amistad: "give us free": A Celebration of the Film by Steven Spielberg*, authors Meredith Maran and Anne McGrath write that the cast had to be "physically, emotionally, culturally, and linguistically prepared to reenact a painful time in history."[6] The chains *were* real. Some of the scenes were so harsh that some cast and crew were moved to tears. The movie boasts a high-class cast with Sir Anthony Hopkins, Morgan Freeman, Matthew McConaughey, and Pete Postlethwaite. The slave who began the rebellion, Cinque, is played by

Djimon Hounsou. John Williams, as always, composed the music, and Janusz Kaminski did the cinematography.

The idea for the movie came from actress and choreographer Debbie Allen who, in 1978, read *Amistad I*, published in June 1970 for the Howard University Press. The book's editors are John A. Williams and Charles F. Harris. This was the first Allen had heard of the event. In 1984, she optioned the rights to William Owens's book, *Black Mutiny: The Revolt on the Schooner Amistad*, which was first published in 1953. Allen continued her show business career for the next 10 years, yet the movie idea was always in the back of her mind. She continued to research the story while considering which director would not shy away from its controversial topic. When she saw *Schindler's List* in 1994, she knew that Steven Spielberg was that director, and he agreed with her that the story must be told. According to the Maran/McGrath book, Spielberg said, "There was one side of my brain saying, wait two, three, or four years before you do this story, because everything you do will be compared to *Schindler's List*. But I've never planned my career and never made good on phantom conversations with myself like that. In the end I do what I think I gotta do."[7]

Allen's 10 years of research provided primary information from court records and newspaper accounts plus the research of historians. This was the information she and Spielberg wanted to use versus the numerous books that by this time had been written on the subject. Recreating the filthy, dehumanizing, and unsanitary conditions of the slave trade, particularly during the voyages, was hard for Allen to witness. For example, those who survived the trip from Africa to Havana were fed and greased down to make them look healthier for selling, and men like Cinque fetched around $450. Prospective buyers sometimes inspected every inch of the African to make sure he or she was healthy enough for the morning-to-night work that lay ahead of them. Incarcerated for almost three years, the men were twice tried and twice found innocent, but the acquittals were overthrown by President Van Buren. The third trial, and third acquittal, was in front of the Supreme Court in February 1841. The case is considered a milestone in American history because it gave abolitionists ammunition for ending slavery. President Martin Van Buren was furious, because he was running for reelection and did not want to anger the southern states who saw the decision as yet another cause for war. But instead of being taken back to their homes, the freed Africans were housed in Farmington, Connecticut, and used by the abolitionists in meetings and rallies. Many of the men tired of being taken from place to place and put on display, often not being allowed to sit with their white companions and often called "savages."[8] When the abolitionists finally saw how depressed the *Amistad* survivors were, they sent them back to Africa in 1842. But it was too late. Their village had been destroyed, and Cinque never again saw his wife and child. He worked as an interpreter in a mission until his death in 1879.

Spielberg is sometimes criticized as making historical films such as *Amistad* and *Schindler's List* to "get his tolerance fix," and even his partner at DreamWorks, David Geffen, said that *Amistad* "was less about slavery than 'about white people saving black people.'"[9] But Spielberg has never chosen his movies according to popular consensus. In the December 1997 issue of *Smithsonian*, Kenneth Turan quotes the director as saying, "While making [*Amistad*], I felt I was telling everyone's story—a story that people of all nationalities and races should know."[10] He has also said that he made the movie, in part, for his seven children, two of whom are African-American. In the November 2005 *Smithsonian,* Turan writes that some of the best and most powerful scenes in the movie are played without dialogue. In his December 1997 review, Ebert writes that *Amistad* and *Schindler's List* are "about the ways good men try to work realistically within an evil system to spare a few of its victims," and the most valuable aspect of *Amistad*, he writes, is that the slaves are given names and identities and not left as "faceless victims"[11] as they are usually portrayed. Unfortunately, writes Ebert, the result of the real *Amistad* trial helped only its defendants and not the millions of slaves in bondage. Amazon.com reviewer Dave McCoy calls the movie Spielberg's "most simplistic, sanitized history lesson,"[12] while Fred Harvey of *The History Place* claims the movie "is a masterpiece of film making providing a thoroughly rewarding entertainment and learning experience."[13] McCoy adds that Spielberg has, once again, turned the movie into an *E.T.* experience with title character Cinque as the "adorable alien: lost, lacking a common language, and trying to find his way home."[14] He calls McConaughey "a grown-up Elliot who tries to communicate complicated ideas, such as geography, by drawing pictures in the sand, or language, by having Cinque mimic his facial expressions."[15] The movie was released in December 1997. With a budget of approximately $40 million, the movie's opening weekend brought in only $4,661,866.

SAVING PRIVATE RYAN

Spielberg moved on to yet another nonfiction story, *Saving Private Ryan*, which takes place during Spielberg's favorite time period, World War II ("the most significant event of the last 100 years"[16]). Unbeknownst to each other, he and Tom Hanks had read the script, which is about a band of soldiers who land at Normandy on June 6, 1944, and then are sent off on a mission to find a Private Ryan, who has recently become the sole surviving son in his family. Knowing that Mrs. Ryan will be receiving death notices for three of her sons, Uncle Sam wants to make sure that she gets her fourth son back home. (Private Ryan was really Sgt. Frederick Niland.) Spielberg didn't want just another Hollywood war movie or another action-adventure movie, but an accurate depiction of "combat from the grunt's p.o.v. as it is fought inch by inch, bullet by bullet, in all its arbitrariness and surreality."[17] He wanted the action to be seen through the eyes of scared young men. Spielberg talked with World War II veterans who had been there, the men who had stormed the beaches and battled the Germans all the way to Paris to free France. The first 25 minutes of the movie depict the beach landings, and it is so difficult to watch that many veterans cried and many could not watch it at all. With his usual attention to detail, when Spielberg heard veterans describe the thousands of dead fish and a lone Bible floating in the water, he added them to the film.

In 1998, Steven Spielberg, Tom Hanks, and their families flew to England, where a Hatfield (in Hertfordshire) countryside village was turned into a French village and a beach in Ireland's County Wexford represented Omaha Beach. (The two families spent their off-hours in Gorey, Ireland, at the Marlfield House Hotel.) About 750 extras were borrowed from the Irish Army, some of whom had worked on Mel Gibson's *Braveheart*, released in 1995. Some real amputees were fitted with plastic limbs that were blown off in the battle scenes. For uniform accuracy, Spielberg located the same company that had made the boots for the real World War II GIs. Many German uniforms were found in London, some original tanks were found in Czechoslovakia, and some original landing boats were found in a California desert. After the 3,000 uniforms and boots were made, they were put through an aging process so they would appear "battle-worn." Since their Irish beach was not as broad as Omaha Beach, Spielberg adjusted the camera lenses to produce the illusion of Omaha. Spielberg wanted the audience to put themselves in the places of those young men and see the horrors through the innocent eyes of a young man who likely had never before been in battle. Those who survived the landing did so only by ignoring the dead and dying all around them. Once they survived, Spielberg wanted the audience to "be" in the Allies' world, to be unaware of what the Germans would do next, to be as surprised as were the characters in the movie. He was inspired by the black-and-white photos taken by Robert Capa for wartime issues of *LIFE* magazine, John Ford's 1942 documentary, *The Battle of Midway*, William Wyler's *Memphis*

Belle: A Story of a Flying Fortress (1944), and Frank Capra's *Why We Fight*, a series about World War II produced between 1943 and 1945. He wanted a newsreel feel to the movie, so he used mostly handheld cameras and toned-down color. He made no storyboards, because he wanted to attack each scene like a newsreel cameraman following soldiers into battle. The effect was achieved to such an extent that the camera's lens was splattered and the camera bounced around just as those used in wartime. He and cameraman Janusz Kaminski used various tricks to get the result they desired: different film stock, stripped lenses, flashed film, and desaturated colors. They also used different shutters and speed changes. Since widescreen movies did not appear until the 1950s, they used the 1.85:1 format because, says Spielberg, it is more like what the human sees. Spielberg credits his editor, Mike Kahn, with attaining these goals. "His rhythms are the best in the world, and he tries to throw the audience off of their expectations,"[18] says Spielberg.

To give his actors a concept of what war is really like, Spielberg hired U.S. Marine Captain Dale Dye (a wounded veteran of three active tours in Vietnam) to help with the accuracy of the movie and to drill the actors. He began by putting them through a 10-day boot camp, which actor Edward Burns says was the worst experience of his life. They hiked in good weather and bad. They began training at five in the morning. They slept on the ground, ate rations, and used a latrine. Their source of heat was tiny metal stoves. And Captain Dye yelled at them all the time. All of this would be hard enough on non-Hollywood types, but these were men used to the best life has to offer, and some of them rebelled. Dye responded, "You're embodying the souls of the fallen comrades who made the world safe for democracy. So you're not going to do that lightly. You're going to know the weaponry, you're going to know the tactics, you're going to know the background, and you're going to know the history."[19] Tom Hanks endured the camp and adopted his character's leadership by encouraging his fellow actors. (The only soldier not put through boot camp was Matt Damon, who played Private Ryan. Spielberg wanted the others to resent him and carry that resentment into their acting in the movie.) Spielberg is known for quick filming, but part of the purpose in doing so on this movie was to keep the actors in character. "I really wanted to keep all of the actors off-balance . . . always . . . in combat . . . under fire . . . in jeopardy. . . . War doesn't give you a break, and I didn't want the producers of *Private Ryan* to give them one either."[20] As with real soldiers, the actors became closer to each other and to their characters. They were so good, in fact, that most scenes were filmed in just three or four takes. Spielberg used no music during battle scenes and very little elsewhere, because he wanted to show that real war is "silent death."[21] "Sure it's grim," says Hanks, "but it's brutally honest."[22] Of course, such movies are fodder for accidents, so Spielberg made sure that only stuntmen were close to the explosives and made sure to use "crack" safety teams and supervisors. Even so, there were some injuries, but the saddest occurrence was when a young actor died in a car crash on his way home.

While Spielberg sees *Saving Private Ryan* as a chance to introduce World War II heroes to today's young people, his main purpose is to honor all veterans, especially his father, with whom he grew closer during the filming. (Trivia: Arnold Spielberg had told his son about an expression they used during the war, "FUBAR: Fouled Up Beyond All Recognition,"[23] and it became part of the script.) When word got out about the opening scene, Spielberg feared that it would keep viewers away. In fact, about halfway through filming, he told his actors not to expect a blockbuster at the box office but to think of what they were making as a tribute. "We're thanking all those guys, your grandparents and my dad, who fought in World War II."[24] In fact, Spielberg and Hanks did such a good job that on Veterans Day, 1999, they were awarded the Distinguished Public Service Award, the Navy's highest civilian honor. The ceremony took place on board the USS *Normandy* in Florida.

Reviews on the movie were mixed. John Simon of the *National Review* writes that Spielberg failed to make his characters come to life and that *Saving Private Ryan* is no better than many other war movies, that, "Only as a catalogue of horrors does *SPR* outdo the rest."[25] Stanley Kauffmann of the *New Republic* agrees. "Steven Spielberg's new film begins as a monumental epic; then it diminishes; and, by its finish, is baffling. . . . Once the Private Ryan mission starts, the picture becomes a good war movie, not much more."[26] On the other hand, *People* magazine writes that *Saving Private Ryan* is about whether it is worth risking one life for another. "Why fight at all? What does any one man owe another? . . . The answers the movie provides are never pat, jingoistic responses about country and duty but rather more complicated ones about friends, family and simple decency."[27] In the end, the review labels the movie as "flat-out great."[28] In *Variety*, Todd McCarthy writes that *Saving Private Ryan* is telling the stories about war "that fathers never tell their families," and that the movie is "second to none as a vivid, realistic and bloody portrait of armed conflict, as well as a generally effective intimate drama about a handful of men on a mission of debatable value in the middle of the war's decisive action."[29] Blogcritics.org writes, "The great power of *Saving Private Ryan* is how it simply presents war and the effect of war on the men who must bear it."[30] Spielberg may have worried that the movie might not appeal to audiences, but he need not have done so. The movie brought in $30 million in its opening weekend, in July 1998. By Christmas, it had made more than $180 million. Neither Spielberg nor Hanks took a salary but rather a share of the movie's gross proceeds. Tom Hanks's biographer David Gardner writes that the money was "an incredible achievement for a 3-hour epic with an R-Restricted rating, no romance and hideous violence."[31] Of the film's success, Spielberg says that he is thrilled. "The people have spoken. They said they were ready to go back a half-century to a blasphemous time and have the courage to experience *Saving Private Ryan*. I think their courage was remarkable."[32] Regarding Spielberg, Hanks says, "Making this movie was like walking into Thomas Edison's laboratory. You're in the presence of this genius who in real life is this badly dressed, nebbishy kinda guy who talks in tangents and only vaguely answers a question. But seeing him on the set, he's a dynamo, a source of incredible vision and information that's hard to keep up with."[33] *Saving Private Ryan* was nominated for 11 Academy Awards and received five, including Best Director, about which Spielberg says, "I never, ever get blasé about this. This day is always indelibly tattooed on the frontal lobe of my brain. I'm usually never nervous about these kinds of things but this always makes me so nervous."[34] Spielberg and Hanks went on to help finance the D-Day Museum in New Orleans and co-produce the World War II television mini-series, *Band of Brothers*, based on the best-selling book by Stephen Ambrose, *Citizen Soldier*.

TOM HANKS

Tom Hanks is someone who knows Steven Spielberg on both professional and personal levels. They first worked together when Amblin produced the Hanks movie, *The Money Pit*, a 1986 slapstick comedy. They found that they had much in common and have been friends ever since. Both are products of divorce. Both live in the same neighborhood and have wives and children who are involved in the same activities. Both had fathers who served in the military during World War II. They mutually admire each other's capabilities and grab onto the better idea, no matter who had it first. In June 2004, they were interviewed together by Barry Koltnow of the *Orange County Register*. When asked what made their relationship work, Spielberg said that it was because they listen to each other, have a mutual respect for each other's opinions, and neither have egos that come into play. This was proven when Hanks wanted the role of Amon Goeth in *Schindler's List* but Spielberg gave it to Ralph Fiennes. Hanks says that Spielberg, "sees things that other directors don't see."[35]

Spielberg appreciates Hanks's "self-deprecating sense of humor."[36] Both men love what they do and feel grateful to be doing it. Says Spielberg of Hanks, "His gratitude for his career is not very common in this business."[37] Spielberg also proudly calls George Lucas a friend. "You know, we've been friends since 1967, and we've never had a fight. It's the longest friendship I've had in my life."[38]

A.I. ARTIFICIAL INTELLIGENCE

In the summer of 2001, Steven Spielberg returned to the world of children with *A.I. Artificial Intelligence*. Told from the main character's point of view, the movie—like so many Spielberg movies—shows a child forced into the cold cruel world. In this case, the little boy is a robot who seeks love and family. Critic Andrew Sarris writes that the movie is a "haunting experience" and "an exquisite work of art."[39] Based on a short story by Brian Aldiss, first published in *Harper's Bazaar* in 1969 as "Supertoys Last All Summer Long," the screen story was written by Ian Watson and the screenplay by Spielberg. Famed director Stanley Kubrick met Steven Spielberg in London in 1979 and asked him to direct his next project, *A.I.* Many people saw the two men as too different to work on the same movie. After all, Kubrick was known for slightly weird films while Spielberg was known for cozy ones. In reality, the two men had some similarities. According to the 2004 book, *Essential Cinema on the Necessity of Film Canons*, by Jonathan Rosenbaum, both men were "Jewish prodigies and technical wizards"[40] who liked science fiction and war movies. After Kubrick's death, Spielberg took on the project, and while he tried to make it in the vein he thought that Kubrick would have wanted, he included his style too. This contrast made the film hard for some critics to categorize and judge instead of just appreciating it for what it was.

The story is about robots that are created to do menial work and evolve into children for couples who cannot get permission to have their own. When a couple's son becomes very ill, they adopt one of the robots and call him David (Haley Joel Osment). But when their son recovers and wants David out of the house, the parents must decide what to do. David's belief in his favorite story, *Pinocchio*, causes him to search for a loving family. According to Patrick Lee of www.scifi.com, "*A.I.* is one of the clearest examples of hard science fiction ever filmed, extrapolating a future based on real science and employing its intriguing premise as a potent metaphor for the human condition."[41] And while the movie fuses Kubrick's "austerity" with Spielberg's "sentimentality," Lee writes that the movie is "moving without being cloying, and thought-provoking without being off-putting."[42] Spielberg's use of atmospheric lighting and John Williams's music, Lee writes, blend with Kubrick's "languid pacing, formal composition and occasionally detached point of view."[43] He adds that Williams's score is sometimes reminiscent of one of Kubrick's favorite composers, Gvorgy Ligeti. Spielberg uses special effects in such a natural way that they seem natural to the story. Lee concludes his review by saying that the movie is bound to become a science fiction classic. Famed movie critic Roger Ebert calls the movie "both wonderful and maddening" because it is "one of the most ambitious films of recent years, filled with wondrous sights and provocative ideas, but it miscalculates in asking us to invest our emotions in a character that is, after all, a machine."[44]

The movie won five awards from the Academy of Science Fiction, Fantasy and Horror Films, USA: Best Music (Williams), Best Performance by a Young Actor (Osment), Best Science Fiction Film, Best Special Effects, and Best Writing (Spielberg). Other actors in the film are Jude Law, William Hurt, Frances O'Connor, Sam Robards, and Brendan Gleeson. At an estimated cost of $90 million to make, the movie opened on July 1, 2001, and made $29,352,630 its first weekend. In April 2006, Carnegie Mellon University announced the robots that will be inducted into their Robot Hall of Fame in June, and "David" was one of them. "In *A.I.*, the android boy David provides an important template for thinking about robot/human relationships," said psychologist Sherry Turkle, director of the MIT Initiative on Technology and Self. "I think that the problem he sets up with his adoptive mother, Monica—that we love the machine we nurture—is a significant model for an important psychological dynamic in contemporary robotics."[45]

NOTES

1. Quoted in Peter Biskind, "A World Apart." *Premiere*, May 1997, reprinted in *Steven Spielberg Interviews*, Lester D. Friedman and Brent Notbohm, eds., (Jackson: University Press of Mississippi, 2000), 197.

2. Ibid.

3. Quoted in Susan Goldman Rubin, *Steven Spielberg: Crazy for Movies* (New York: Harry N. Abrams, 2001), 66.

4. Quoted in Biskind, 200–201.

5. Joseph McBride, "*The Lost World Jurassic Park*." www.boxoffice.com (accessed May 2, 2006).

6. Meredith Maran and Anne McGrath, eds., *Amistad: "give us free."* A *Celebration of the Film by Steven Spielberg* (New York: Newmarket Press, 1998), 49–50.

7. Quoted in Maran, 16.

8. Quoted in Maran, 36.

9. Quoted in Stephen J. Dubner, "Steven the Good." *The New York Times* magazine, February 14, 1999, reprinted in *Steven Spielberg Interviews*, Lester D. Friedman and Brent Notbohm, eds. (Jackson: University Press of Mississippi, 2000), 235.

10. Quoted in Kenneth Turan, "Steven Spielberg," *Smithsonian*, November 2005, 110.

11. Roger Ebert, "*Amistad*," December 12, 1997. www.rogerebert.suntimes. com.

12. Dave McCoy, "Review of *Amistad* (1997)." www.amazon.com (undated electronic work).

13. Fred Harvey, Review of *Amistad*, The History Place, December 20, 1997, www.historyplace.com.

14. Harvey.

15. McCoy.

16. Quoted in Stephen Pizzello, "Five-Star General," *American Cinematographer*, August 1998, reprinted in *Steven Spielberg Interviews*, Lester D. Friedman and Brent Notbohm, eds. (Jackson: University Press of Mississippi, 2000), 208.

17. John Simon, Review of *Amistad*, *National Review*, December 31, 1997.

18. Quoted in Pizzello, 213.

19. Quoted in Rubin, 82.

20. Quoted in Pizzello, 214.

21. Quoted in Rubin, 85.

22. Quoted in David Gardner, *Tom Hanks: The Unauthorized Biography* (London: Blake, 1999), 200.

23. Quoted in Rubin, 85.

24. Quoted in Kenneth Turan, "Crossroads: Steven Spielberg," *Los Angeles Times*, December 28, 1998, reprinted in *Steven Spielberg Interviews*, Lester D. Friedman and Brent Notbohm, eds. (Jackson: University Press of Mississippi, 2000), 222.

25. John Simon, "Review of *Saving Private Ryan*," *National Review*, August 17, 1998, 52(1). www.web7.infotrac.galegroup.com.

26. Stanley Kauffmann, "*Saving Private Ryan*," *New Republic*, August 17, 1998, 24(1). www.web7.infotrac.galegroup.com.

27. *People Weekly*, "Reviews of *Saving Private Ryan*," August 3, 1998, 25(1). www.web7.infotrac.galegroup.com.

28. Ibid.

29. Todd McCarthy, Review of *Saving Private Ryan*, *Variety*, July 20, 1998, 45(1). www.web7.infotrac.galegroup.com.

30. Samuel James, Review of *Saving Private Ryan*, May 27, 2006. www. blogcritics.org.

31. Gardner, 203.

32. Quoted in Gardner, 204.

33. Quoted in Gardner, 205.

34. Quoted in Gardner, 204.

35. Quote in Barry Koltnow, "The Misfits: Hanks and Spielberg never fit in—which is why they're friends," *Orange County Register*, June 16, 2004. www. infotrac.galegroup.com.

36. Quoted in Koltnow.

37. Ibid.

38. Quoted in Sean Smith, "King of the Worlds; Spielberg Talks about Movies, Terror and Wonder, and Why the *Oprah* Thing Bothered Him—But Only a Little." *Newsweek.* June 27, 2005, 58. www.web2.infotrac.galegroup.com.

39. Quoted in Rubin, 86.

40. Jonathan Rosenbaum, *Essential Cinema: On the Necessity of Film Canons* (Baltimore: Johns Hopkins University Press, 2004), 272.

41. Patrick Lee, "*A.I. Artificial Intelligence.*" www.scifi.com (accessed January 30, 2006).

42. Ibid.

43. Ibid.

44. Roger Ebert, "*A.I. Artificial Intelligence,*" June 29, 2001. www.rogerebert. suntimes.com.

45. Carnegie Mellon University Department of Media Relations, "Carnegie Mellon University Announces 2006 Inductees Into Robot Hall of Fame," April 19, 2006. www.roboticonline.com.

Chapter 7

THE LEGEND CONTINUES, 2002–2005

MINORITY REPORT

Spielberg's next project, *Minority Report*, finally brought him together with Tom Cruise. Both men had long wanted to work together, and moviegoers had long wanted to see what magic the two would produce. Based on the 1956 short story by Philip K. Dick, the story was adapted and updated to the year 2054. A science fiction and detective story in one, *Minority Report* is about a group of investigators who try to prevent crimes by arresting the potential perpetrators before they commit the crime. Spielberg has long been intrigued with the idea of knowing the future. Although the movie was a winner at the box office, it received mixed reviews. On *Variety*'s Web site, critic Todd McCarthy writes that there was not enough action for thrill seekers yet it was not different enough for "highbrows."[1] He also writes that the movie was Spielberg's "darkest and most socially relevant"[2] but did not have the box office appeal expected of a Spielberg/ Cruise combination. On the other hand, *Times* critic Richard Corliss writes that the movie *did* achieve the balance between the thrill seekers and highbrows and is Spielberg's best "entertainment film"[3] since *Raiders of the Lost Ark*. Roger Ebert writes that *Minority Report* shows Spielberg at his best. He calls the movie a "triumph" and "a film that works on our minds and our emotions."[4] J. Hoberman of the *Village Voice* thinks the movie is entertaining and the "least pretentious genre movie Steven Spielberg has made in the decade since *Jurassic Park*."[5] But Hoberman likes the sweetness for which Spielberg is known and prefers that the director stay away from social commentary. Peter Travers of the *Rolling Stone* praises the acting of Colin Farrell, Tom Cruise, and Samantha Morton, and says that the movie is "laced with dark humor and powered by a topical idea."[6] He writes that Spielberg uses technology and suspense to its best, but that the ending is too predictable and that the film raises moral questions but does not answer them. "Final report: Good, yes; great, no."[7] Writing for scifi.com, Cindy White calls *Minority Report* "that rare kind of high-concept film that marries a well-told story with eye-popping visual effects. Engaging from the very first scene, it grabs the audience and never lets go."[8] *Minority Report's* budget was approximately $102 million. In its opening weekend of June 23, 2002, it made $35,677,125; and by October 2002, its gross proceeds in the United States were $132,014,112. The film was nominated for one Academy Award and won four Saturns, including Best Picture, from the Academy of Science Fiction, Fantasy and Horror Films, USA.

CATCH ME IF YOU CAN

From a futuristic drama, Spielberg went back in time to the 1960s for a comedy/drama, *Catch Me If You Can*, which came out during the Christmas season of 2002 and starred two of Hollywood's best: Tom Hanks and Leonardo DiCaprio. The idea came about when DreamWorks bought the story by Frank W. Abagnale, Jr., a man who had successfully passed himself off as an airline pilot, a lawyer, and a doctor—all before the age of 21. As he read the story, Spielberg says that it was easy to see how Abagnale's charm made it possible to pull off his hoaxes. "I have always loved movies about sensational rogues—they break the law, but you just have to love them for their moxie."[9] The director likes DiCaprio's creativity and his striving for perfection, and DiCaprio likes Spielberg's ability to bring out the best in his actors. One reason that Hanks signed on to play Carl Hanratty, the FBI agent who tracks down Abagnale and finally catches him, is because Hanratty recognizes the sadness and potential in the young man. He sees him as someone who is redeemable and, sure enough, Abagnale serves his time and then becomes a member of the FBI. As do most of his movies, *Catch Me If You Can* appealed to Spielberg's own history. The young Abagnale was a child of the 1960s who was raised in a suburban neighborhood and heartbroken when his parents divorced. He was so torn by the divorce and trying to decide which parent he should live with that he ran away. When he made a lot of money, he thought it would bring his parents back together and impress his father (Christopher Walken), who is charming but broke. The fact that Abagnale was not an adult when he performed his amazing stunts is another familiar Spielberg trait: boys forced into manhood. "This story," says Spielberg, "could only have taken place in an age of innocence . . . in the sixties there was a community of trust. That innocence was something all of us are nostalgic about."[10] Not only did the plot remind Spielberg of his parents' divorce but also the fabled story of his time spent on the Universal lot when he was just a teenager (see chapter 1).

The story was sold for movie rights before it was written. When Frank Abagnale, Jr., appeared on various talk/news programs, audiences requested his book, but there was no book. He sold his story in 1978 to producer Bud Yorkin, who optioned it to producer Hall Bartlett in 1986. The story and its various screenplays bounced around the movie industry until Abagnale decided that he wanted it back if Bartlett did not agree to purchase it. By selling it to Bartlett for around $250,000, Abagnale lost control over his story and earned no more money from it. As happens in Hollywood, the story bounced around some more even after DreamWorks purchased it. But as soon as DiCaprio signed on to the project, it picked up momentum. Spielberg gave Abagnale a cameo spot in the film and hired him as a consultant. DiCaprio spent time with Abagnale to learn his habits and mannerisms. He was amazed at the man's subtlety, eye contact, charm, energy, and intelligence combined with the appearance of success and power. When Abagnale saw that both stars and the director were genuinely concerned with making a good movie, he once again grew excited about his own story.

The magic of good moviemaking is often subtle, and this movie is full of details that the audience does not realize it sees. The 1960s are everywhere—bold colors, stylish clothes—and it was the era when merchandise became glamorous, when people were glamorous and dressed up to attend a movie or go out to eat. In *Catch Me If You Can*, the clothes and sets become brighter as DiCaprio's character grows bolder. DiCaprio, who likes period films because they give so much freedom, had 100 wardrobe changes. The movie's production designer, Jeannine Oppewall, says that the film started out with 186 sets. "We shot in 60 days in two countries, four metropolitan areas—most days it felt more like running a marathon than designing a film."[11] But her crew did such a good job that it won the Excellence in Production Design for a Contemporary Film Award from the Art Directors Guild in 2003. Christopher Walken and John Williams were nominated for Academy Awards, and Walken won the Best Supporting Actor Award from the British Academy of Film and Television Arts Awards (BAFTA), the Screen Actors Guild (SAG), and the National Society of Film Critics Award, USA (NSFC). Usually typecast as cold and cruel, Walken shines as a hapless but loving father figure to DiCaprio.

Spielberg says that Walken "has some of the best natural instincts of anyone I've worked with."[12] In his December 23, 2002, movie review in the *New Yorker*, David Denby calls it a true holiday film. *Catch Me If You Can* opened on December 29, 2002. At an estimated cost of $52 million to make, it made $30,082,000 in its first weekend. By April 20, 2003, the movie had grossed $164,435,221. Spielberg says that making the movie was like "a breath of fresh air."[13]

THE TERMINAL

Spielberg and Hanks teamed up again for *The Terminal*. Two other members of the ensemble cast are Catherine Zeta-Jones and Stanley Tucci. Hanks plays Viktor Navorski, a citizen from the tiny European county of Krakozhia, who has come to the United States to keep a promise to his deceased father. He has barely arrived at JFK Airport before he learns that his country has gone through upheaval and no longer exists, which means that he no longer has a home country, and his passport is no longer valid. He cannot leave the airport. As always, Hanks plays the innocent and naïve character beautifully, and his first moments of trying to discern what has happened are quite sad. He does not need pity, however, as he is probably the most resourceful person alive. While he continues daily attempts to get a visa, he becomes friends with the airport staff and even finds ways to make money for food. There is even the hint at a romance with Zeta-Jones. The airport, says Spielberg, is still "the only place where the melting pot theory still works, when you're stuck with each other, waiting in line,"[14] and the cacophony of sights and sounds becomes Viktor's America. *Saint Paul Pioneer Press* reviewer Chris Hewitt writes that when Viktor yearningly gazes outside the huge plate-glass windows, "America remains a place of hope and possibility."[15] As with *Catch Me If You Can*, *The Terminal* paid amazing attention to detail. Production designer Alex McDowell created an entire world for Viktor inside an airport terminal, and Spielberg tried to film it all. For example, there is a scene where Viktor is starving so he makes himself a sandwich of crackers and catsup. The holes in the crackers were purposely made larger so that enough catsup would seep through to provide an image of a "pop art painting."[16] Hewitt sums up the movie. "The hoped-for effect is a stop-and-smell-the-Starbucks experience for Viktor, and for audiences, because great things can happen while you're waiting for whatever you're waiting for."[17] While the *New Yorker* writes that Spielberg did not "exploit the situation of a trapped man for the desperate nightmare that it really is,"[18] Philip Wuntch of the *Dallas Morning News* calls the movie "joyous" and writes, "It confirms Steven Spielberg as a personal filmmaker and Tom Hanks as an inventive comic actor."[19] The Art Directors Guild awarded their Excellence in Production Design Award to Alex McDowell and his crew; and BMI Film & TV Awards gave their Film Music Award to John Williams. The movie opened on September 9, 2004, and made $77,872,883 in that first weekend. It cost approximately $60 million to make.

WAR OF THE WORLDS

Steven Spielberg and Tom Cruise teamed up again in the $128 million remake of the 1953 *War of the Worlds*. (Trivia: Two stars of the earlier film, Gene Barry and Ann Robinson, make cameo appearances.) But why a remake at all? In 1953, the United States and the Soviet Union were in a Cold War that so scared people that many built fallout shelters, and school children routinely practiced duck-and-cover drills. Everyone lived in constant fear of nuclear war, which made the era ripe for science fiction movies about creatures transformed into monsters due to radioactive fallout and about creatures from outer space. With the attack on the United States by terrorists on September 11, 2001, Spielberg believed that it was time for a remake, but with some changes. As Owen Gleiberman writes in his review for *Entertainment Weekly*, what scares the 2005 audience is not the alien itself but the "fiery fulfillment of our collective nervousness about the fate of the future."[20] Spielberg says that such movies also show that human beings come together when there is a common enemy. Carina Chocano, a film critic for the *Los Angeles Times*, writes about the obvious references to September 11: "Terrified residents rush through the streets covered in ash and dust; handmade missing-person posters line the sidewalks; commercial airliners fall from the sky, to be instantly scavenged by predatory news media; pieces of clothing rain down from above."[21] Even Dakota Fanning's character asks, "Is it the terrorists?"[22]

Cruise was anxious to play a blue-collar father figure instead of his usual bigger-than-life hero. While Anthony L. Cuaycong writes in the July 1, 2005, issue of *BusinessWorld Manila* that Tom Cruise's "star power . . . prevents him from being anything but heroic,"[23] Owen Gleiberman writes that the time was right for Cruise to play the part because he has been around long enough and is old enough not to play a hero but a dad who loves his kids but has not been a good parent. Unlike most science fiction movies made in the 1950s, this one does not show scientists or politicians, something that the *New Yorker*'s David Denby misses. But Spielberg omitted them on purpose, opting for a story about one family's survival. Executive Producer Paula Wagner says that the story shows that human beings are sometimes more dangerous to themselves than are extraterrestrial invaders—and one that shows that a father's most important job is being the best father he can be. As always, Spielberg knows that using the "everyman" character allows the audience to relate to the movie. The movie also stars Tim Robbins as survivalist Harlan, Justin Chatwin as Cruise's son Robbie, and Dakota Fanning as daughter Rachel. Soren Andersen writes about Fanning's effect on the movie in his review for the Tacoma, Washington, *News Tribune*. "Steven Spielberg puts Fanning's azure orbs front and center in the frame to drive home the human dimension of the threatened extermination of humanity. It's an effective strategy."[24] The U.S. Marines in the movie are real. The tanks they use are real. Spielberg asked them how they would actually react in such a situation and then listened and utilized what he could of their response. After their scenes were completed, the director posed for pictures with them and thanked them with huge cakes.

Storyboards were used to help cast and crew know what to expect and when. Especially when using special effects, the actors need to know how to react to digital images that they cannot see. Spielberg worked closely with Dan Gregoire, the previsualization supervisor, and the art department to make sure that all the ideas were going to work before they were filmed—much less expensive than wasting film. Along the same line, scenes requiring digital effects were filmed first so that the special-effects people could work on them while the rest of the movie was being made. Likewise, scenes filmed on the East Coast were shot first so the West Coast sets would be ready when needed. Although there was a rush to get the movie out, Spielberg did not skip on anything that would improve the picture. Tom Cruise says, "He really understands storytelling and what's important."[25] Cruise also says that it is a tribute to Spielberg's storytelling ability that the actors and story "work" even before the special effects are added. Spielberg says that he never wants to do an all green-set movie because he gets new ideas when he walks onto a new set. He fears that building real sets is becoming a lost art, and that eventually there will be entire movies made via computer imagery with no physical or emotional contact with anyone. "Now that terrifies me," he says. "It crosses a moral boundary to me. . . . Collaboration is what makes being a director an electrifying experience."[26] Spielberg did not want *War of the Worlds* to look like science fiction, so he kept the lighting as natural as possible to obtain the most realistic look. Spielberg's crew has been together for many years because they work so well together. His director of photography, Janusz Kaminski, ASC, says that Spielberg's talent kept the film from feeling "over stylized."[27] Other *War of the Worlds* crew members are Production

Designer Rick Carter, Composer John Williams, Special Effects Expert Dennis Muren, and Stunt Coordinator Vic Armstrong. Spielberg filmed the crowd scenes first, as he usually does, to get the adrenaline flowing and to build momentum. Filming on the East Coast with its freezing temperatures was pretty miserable, especially those scenes filmed on the water, but the local extras were very good-natured. They portrayed the citizens trying to escape the aliens by getting on a ferryboat. Now refugees, they wore multilayers because they could take only what they could wear and carry. The actual boat sequences were digitized or filmed in a tank in Los Angeles. The boat was real but smaller than a normal ferryboat. In another scene, a plane crashes and its engine falls into Cruise's character's house. Spielberg had to buy and then destroy a real airplane for the sequence. He wants lasting images in his movies, something audience members will not forget. In this case, it is the image of a 747 crashing into an ordinary neighborhood. Throughout the movie, Spielberg purposely shows no body parts. This goes back to his *Jaws* days, when he learned that less is more. By not showing body parts, Spielberg says that the audience will "see things that aren't really there."[28] *Hindu Businessline's* Shyam G. Menon writes that once the first tripod (the alien) appears, "The next 10 minutes is gripping footage shot through a panic-stricken camera. Such deliberate camera work and retention of a human atmosphere runs through the entire film, giving a classical touch to the exhausted work of sci-fi imagery." Spielberg is able, writes Menon, "to give personality to aliens."[29] Gleiberman writes that the aliens seem like something from dreams, a terror that "is far away and close up at the same time, which may be why the movie collides so forcefully with our anxieties."[30] Spielberg also uses, writes Gleiberman, the same "stop-and-go rhythm of foreboding threat"[31] that he used in *Jaws* and *Saving Private Ryan*. In his review for the *Wall Street Journal*, Joe Morgenstern writes that "the movie provides a plethora of pitiless aliens, with their destructive, tripod-shaped machines" that create "a planetary hell."[32]

Does Spielberg think there are aliens? Yes, ever since he got his first telescope and began searching the night sky. "This movie's been a real trip for me," he says. "It's the first time I've really jumped with both eyes open and both feet directly into the center of a science fiction horror film."[33] (He says that he still wants to make a real science fiction movie where nothing is earthly.) Producer Kathleen Kennedy says that *War of the Worlds* might be seen as the third—and darkest part—of a *Close Encounters-E.T.* trilogy, that "the edgier darker story has always been somewhere inside him."[34] Tom Cruise calls *War of the Worlds* "*E.T.* gone bad."[35] A. O. Scott of the *The New York Times* writes that the movie is "a reminder that Mr. Spielberg . . . is still capable, 30 years after *Jaws*, of making really scary movies."[36] Morgenstern writes that "Spielberg has put the summer back in summer movies."[37] Made at an estimated budget of $132 million *War of the Worlds* made $77,061,953 in its opening weekend (July 4, 2005) and $234,280,354 by that November. It received three Academy Award nominations, and Dakota Fanning won a Saturn for the Best Performance by a Younger Actor from the Academy of Science Fiction, Fantasy, and Horror Films USA.

MUNICH

War of the Worlds was one of two Spielberg movies nominated for 2006 Academy Awards. The host of the awards, comedian Jon Stewart, had fun with the famous director. "Steven Spielberg is here. . . . A best-director nomination for *Munich*, a tremendous film, and I congratulate you, sir. From the man who also gave us *Schindler's List. Schindler's List* and *Munich*. I think I speak for all Jews when I say I can't wait to see what happens to us next. Trilogy!"[38] Spielberg remembers watching the 1972 Olympics when 11 Israeli team members were kidnapped and executed by the Palestinian terrorist group Black September. *Munich* tells the story of the Israelis who pursued and killed those terrorists at the direction of Israeli Prime Minister Golda Meir. Five men were chosen to carry out the order called the "Wrath of God," and eventually 10 Palestinians were killed. In an article for the *Los Angeles Times*, Rachel Abramowitz writes that Israel still has not "formally claimed responsibility"[39] and that the subject is still a sore one in the country. In his review for the *The New York Times*, David M. Halbfinger writes that by making the movie, Spielberg "could jeopardize his tremendous stature among Jews both in the United States and in Israel."[40] Since he did not want to be the cause of any problems in the Middle East, the director sought advice from former president Bill Clinton, former American diplomat Dennis Ross, former White House spokesman Mike McCurry, and Hollywood spokesman and crisis communicator Allan Mayer. Spielberg is always secretive about upcoming projects and was even more so with *Munich*, but in hopes of lessening any problems, he sent simultaneous short statements to the *The New York Times*, *Ma'ariv* (an Israeli newspaper), and *Al Arabiya* (an Arab television network).

Co-producer Barry Mendel is also someone who remembers the 1972 Olympics, and when he saw a documentary about the revenge taken by the Israelis, he knew that it would be a great story. To learn more, he read different accounts but was most fascinated by George Jonas's *Vengeance: The True Story of an Israeli Counter-Terrorist Team*, first published in 1984. Although Mendel says that the book's information cannot be proven, Jonas's source is supposed to be one of the five members of the actual revenge team. And because Spielberg is always more interested in the human element, it is these men who are the focus of *Munich*. The result, writes *Seattle Times* movie critic Moira Macdonald, is a "smart, mesmerizing and often angry film,"[41] and that Spielberg shows the humanity in every character in the movie. *Munich* is another of Spielberg's movies in which he did not depend on storyboards because he wanted every day to be new. One of the movie's stars, Daniel Craig, says that it is obvious that Spielberg loves actors by the way he responds to their suggestions and takes advantage of unexpected moments. Another one of the stars, Eric Bana, agrees and was surprised at how easily Spielberg would change a shot if it meant making a better movie. On Universal's *Munich* Web site, cinematographer Janusz Kaminski says how easy it is for him to work with Spielberg, that after making 10 movies together, they have established trust and understanding. He comments that in *Munich* Spielberg once again shows his genius for using the camera to create atmosphere. In this case, it is suspense made by using reflections in cars and around corners. Spielberg also incorporated the footage of the old actual news footage, which Barry Mendel collected, thinking that it would "ground this movie in realism as nothing else possibly could."[42]

While *Munich* was nominated for five Academy Awards, the movie and its director came under fire from some for being anti-Semitic and from others for a controversial bedroom scene. Laura King, Jerusalem Bureau Chief for the *Los Angeles Times*, wrote her review from Jerusalem, where the movie was not drawing very big crowds. Israel still carries out targeted assassinations, writes King, and some in Israel's spy organization have not been pleased with the movie. Although *Entertainment Weekly*'s Owen Gleiberman criticizes the movie for some of its content, he called *Munich*, "spectacularly gripping and unsettling . . . grave and haunted . . . yet its power lies in its willingness to be a work of brutal excitement."[43] Spielberg's camera seems "to be everywhere at once" and "John Williams' score is like a telltale heartbeat."[44] One scene is even called "Hitchcockian"[45] yet the characters are made human with their humor and nitpicking. Roger Ebert calls the movie "an act of courage and conscience."[46] Spielberg and his producers want the movie to ignite discussions about how to deal with terrorism and hope that the movie shows that no matter which response is taken, there will be consequences. More than anything else, Spielberg wants the movie to be an honor to the fallen athletes so they will never be forgotten. Made at an estimated cost of $75 million, *Munich* made $6,040,860 in its opening weekend of December 25, 2005. By March 26, 2006, the movie had grossed $47,379,090.

NOTES

1. Todd McCarthy, Review of *Minority Report*, www.variety.com, reprinted in *Film Studies*, Warren Buckland, ed. Teach Yourself, 2nd ed., Series (Chicago: McGraw-Hill, 2003), 165.

2. Ibid.

3. Richard Corliss, "No Artificial Intelligence; Just Smart Fun," *Time*, November 1, 2002, reprinted in *Film Studies*, Warren Buckland, ed. Teach Yourself, 2nd ed., Series (Chicago: McGraw-Hill, 2003), 171.

4. Roger Ebert, "Review of *Minority Report*," Chicago Sun-Times online, June 6, 2002, reprinted in *Film Studies*, Warren Buckland, ed. Teach Yourself, 2nd ed., Series (Chicago: McGraw-Hill, 2003), 172.

5. J. Hoberman, "Private Eyes," *Village Voice*, February 16, 2002, reprinted in *Film Studies*, Warren Buckland, ed. Teach Yourself, 2nd ed., Series (Chicago: McGraw-Hill, 2003), 169.

6. Peter Travers, Review of *Minority Report*, *Rolling Stone*, July 18, 2002. www.rollingstone.com.

7. Ibid.

8. Cindy White, "Review of *Minority Report*," www.scifi.com (accessed January 30, 2006).

9. Quoted in Nestor U. Torre, "DiCaprio, Hanks and Spielberg Work Well Together," *Philippine Daily Inquirer*, Asia Africa Intelligence Wire, February 1, 2003. www.web7.infotrac.galegroup.com.

10. Quoted in *Catch Me If You Can: A Steven Spielberg Film*. Introduction by Frank W. Abagnale (New York: Newmarket Press, 2002), 13.

11. Quoted in Lisa Hirsch, "Design Kudos *Catch* hobbits, (Art Directors Guilds Production Design Awards Banquet)." *Daily Variety*, February 24, 2003, 4(2). www.find.galegroup.com.

12. Quoted in Tom Sinclair, "Christopher Walken: *Catch Me If You Can*," *Entertainment Weekly*, February 21, 2003, 45. www.find.galegroup.com.

13. Quoted in *Catch Me If You Can*, "Bonus Features." DVD, directed by Steven Spielberg. Universal City, CA: Dreamworks Home Entertainment, 2002.

14. Quoted in Chris Hewitt, "Spielberg's *The Terminal*: Pay Attention to the Nuts," *Saint Paul Pioneer Press* (via Knight-Ridder/Tribune News Service), June 14, 2004. www.infotrac.galegroup.com.

15. Ibid.

16. Ibid.

17. Ibid.

18. David Denby, "Wanderers: The Current Cinema," *New Yorker*, July 5, 2004, 99–101. www.proquest.umi.com.

19. Philip Wuntch, "*The Terminal*," *Dallas Morning News* (via Knight-Ridder/Tribune News Service), June 15, 2004. www.infotrac.galegroup.com.

20. Owen Gleiberman, Review of *Munich*, *Entertainment Weekly*, January 17, 2006. www.ew.com.

21. Carina Chocano, "Movies: The Director's Art: To think like the masters; For Steven Spielberg, it takes a vicious alien attack to restore dad as the head of the family," *Los Angeles Times*, July 10, 2005, E1. www.proquest.umi.com.

22. Quoted in Chocano.

23. Anthony L. Cuaycong, "Courtside," *BusinessWorld Manila*, July 1, 2005, 1. www.proquest.umi.com.

24. Soren Andersen, "*War* wins some battles: Steven Spielberg's take on H.G. Wells's *War of the Worlds* is effectively scary but breaks no new ground," *The News Tribune* (Tacoma, WA), July 1, 2005, South Sound Edition, F24. www.proquest.umi.com.

25. Quoted in "We are not alone," Special Features, *War of the Worlds* DVD, directed by Steven Spielberg. 2-disc limited edition. Universal City, CA: DreamWorks Home Entertainment. 2005.

26. Quoted in Sean Smith, "The King of the World, Spielberg talks about movies, terror and wonder, and why the Oprah thing bothered him—but only a little," *Newsweek*, June 27, 2005, 58. www.infotrac.galegroup.com.

27. Quoted in "We are not alone."

28. Ibid.

29. Shyam G. Menon, "*War of the Worlds*—a great spectacle," *Businessline*, Chennai, July 1, 2005, 1. www.proquest.umi.com.

30. Gleiberman.

31. Ibid.

32. Joe Morgenstern, "Spielberg Comes Home; In Intense *War of the Worlds*, Family Values Trump Effects; Cruise and Dakota Fanning Anchor a Surprisingly Human Drama; *Beat* Reinvents a Cult Classic," *Wall Street Journal*, Weekend Journal, Eastern Edition, July 1, 2005, W1. www.proquest.com.

33. "We are not alone."

34. Quoted in "We are not alone."

35. Ibid.

36. A.O. Scott, "The Boys of Summer: 30 Years Later," *The New York Times*, late edition, East Coast, July 10, 2005, 2.18. www.proquest.umi.com.

37. Morgenstern.

38. *USA Today*, "Some of Jon Stewart's Oscar Lines," March 5, 2006. www.azcentral.com/, accessed Aug 25, 2006.

39. Rachel Abramowitz, "*War* over, Spielberg moves on; As his blockbuster takes theaters, he's wrapped up in the aftermath of the '72 Munich killings," *Los Angeles Times*, July 1, 2005, E1. www.proquest.umi.com.

40. David M. Halbfinger, "Next: Spielberg's Biggest Gamble," *The New York Times*, July 1, 2005, E1. www.proquest.umi.com.

41. Moira Macdonald, "*Munich*: A story of murder and unfathomable vengeance," *Seattle Times*, December 23, 2005. www.seattletimes.newsource.com.

42. *Munich* Web site, www.munichmovie.com (accessed March 11, 2006).

43. Gleiberman.

44. Ibid.

45. Ibid.

46. Roger Ebert, "Review of *Munich*," December 23, 2005. www.rogerebert. suntimes.com.

Chapter 8

AWARDS AND FAME, GOOD WORKS, FUTURE PROJECTS, ACCLAIM

AWARDS

Steven Spielberg has been a major motion picture force since the release of *Jaws* in 1975. In 2006, both *Munich* and *War of the Worlds* were nominated for a total of eight Academy Awards. Although neither movie won an Oscar, eight of Spielberg's movies have received a total of 28 Academy Awards: *Jaws, Close Encounters of the Third Kind, Raiders of the Lost Ark, E.T. the Extra-Terrestrial, Indiana Jones and the Last Crusade, Jurassic Park, Schindler's List,* and *Saving Private Ryan.* He has also directed nine actors in Oscar-nominated performances, although none has yet to win under his watch: Liam Neeson, Ralph Fiennes, Anthony Hopkins, Tom Hanks, Melinda Dillon, Whoopi Goldberg, Oprah Winfrey, Margaret Avery, and Christopher Walken. And when the American Film Institute (AFI) chose its top 100 movies, five of Spielberg's made the top 75: *Schindler's List* (#9), *E.T. the Extra-Terrestrial* (#25), *Jaws* (#48), *Raiders of the Lost Ark* (#60), and *Close Encounters of the Third Kind* (#64).

Spielberg himself has received numerous awards, including, in 1998, "the *Bundesverdienstkreuz mit Stern* (the highest civil distinction the Federal Republic of Germany has to give away) for his sensible representation of Germany's history in his movie *Schindler's List* (1993)."[1] In 2004, he was made a knight of the Legion of Honor of France by President Jacques Chirac and also received the Cavaliere di Gran Croce, Italy's highest award, "for his work to preserve Holocaust history through his films."[2] In May 2005, he was inducted into the Science Fiction Museum and Hall of

Fame (SFM) in Seattle, Washington. In July 2006, he was honored at the 42nd Chicago International Film Festival with the Gold Hugo Lifetime Achievement Award "in recognition of his outstanding 33-year career in the film industry."[3] On November 20, 2006, in New York City, he received the International Emmy Founders Award at the 34th International Emmy Awards Gala. This award "is presented for outstanding work that crosses cultural boundaries and reflects the commonality of the human experience."[4] He ended 2006 by being honored on December 26 at the Kennedy Center Celebration of the Performing Arts.

FAME

Steven Spielberg's very name is used to exemplify movies, power, and wealth. Dominic Wills, Tiscali Entertainment, even wrote that "Spielberg is now a kind of cinematic brand-name."[5] An online *Business Week* article used him to show the desirability of the RX 400h Lexus: "You've gotta figure Steven Spielberg can afford to buy any kind of car he pleases. So, it says something that he and many other Hollywood luminaries have rushed out to buy the new Lexus RX 400h . . ."[6] In a feature about expensive cowboy boots at www.forbes.com, Neal Santelmann writes that John Williams ordered a pair of boots for Spielberg—with inlaid color images of Spielberg, his wife, and their seven children. *Charlotte Observer* critic Lawrence Toppman writes about a documentary about Hurricane Katrina: "She had more impact than any Hollywood power players, from George Lucas to Steven Spielberg . . ."[7] And it is almost impossible to watch much television without seeing spoofs of Spielberg's work. More than 100 shows are listed as doing so at www.imdb.com. A *Daily News Tribune* Web site article tells of Amon Shorr, a young moviemaker who helped found the SurDeis Film Festival. Shorr became enamored with movies when he was 10 years old and saw *Jurassic Park*. "It was the first time I realized where movies come from," he said.[8] Like Spielberg, Shorr began making films when he was in the eighth grade with his father's camera. He is just one of the people Spielberg has inspired. Another person Spielberg has influenced is especially important to him—his son with Amy Irving, Max, who is now 21. Max has worked as a designer for the movie *Trespasser* (1998), a miscellaneous crew member for *The Rage: Carrie 2* (1999), and an actor in *Catch Me If You Can* (2002). When he was 17, he attended a filmmaking workshop run by the New York Film Academy and wrote, produced, directed, shot, and edited his first movie, *Snap Shot*. (The movie is not expected to be released to the public.)

DOWNSIDE OF FAME

Being successful can create expensive, disagreeable, and even nightmarish situations. In addition to those in the media who are handsomely paid to stalk celebrities, there are numerous individuals and Web sites devoted to spotting them and telling the world where they were and what they were doing. Spielberg was even stalked by a man who threatened to rape him. Although the man was sentenced to 25 years to life, the director is now forced to maintain tight security wherever he goes. And there are other problems. After Spielberg and DreamWorks acquired the movie rights to a new novel, *How Opal Mehta Got Kissed, Got Wild and Got A Life*, by Kaavya Viswanathan, they found out in 2006 that the work was plagiarized from another book. Then there was the very successful television mini-series, *Into the West*, which Spielberg produced for TNT in 2005. Not only did some of the Native American extras file complaints against DreamWorks, saying that they had endured hardship conditions, but in 2006, the father of one of the girls filed a $325,000 lawsuit against Turner Films and the movie's hairstylist saying that his daughter's hair was cut, which went against tribal customs.

Success also breeds jealousy. Spielberg is often thought of as being "aloof," "demanding," and even "vaguely unpleasant."[9] But for those who know him well, these are just the rants of people who are envious or who do not know him personally. "I'm not a bully," he says, "and I don't give orders. I'm very collaborative, but what I try to do is inspire in people who are collaborating that they've got to collaborate with me better than they have ever collaborated with anybody before. And so in that sense I'm demanding. I expect the best of anybody who works here."[10] Producer and friend Kathleen Kennedy says that much of the criticism is because he is impatient. He thinks so far ahead that everyone else seems to lag behind. Because of this, he demands that his crew does exactly what he says so no time is wasted and he does not lose the vision in his head. Kennedy also thinks that Spielberg has trouble communicating his feelings and trusting people and wonders if part of it is a desire to be alone with his creative side, in which he is most comfortable.

GOOD WORKS

Along with his numerous film awards, Spielberg has been recognized for his philanthropic work. Even before *Jaws*, he gave the contest awards and net proceeds from his home movies to charities and his high school. When he began making really big money, he began making really big contributions. In 1985, he donated $100,000 to the Planetary Society for its Mega-channel Extraterrestrial Assay system that Harvard's telescope uses "to detect radio signals from distant civilizations."[11] He also serves on its board of directors. His donation to pediatric medicine at the Cedars-Sinai Medical Center in West Hollywood was so significant that there is now a Steven Spielberg Pediatric Research Center in the Steven Spielberg Building. He gave the University of Southern California the money to create a scoring stage for "first-time producers, writers, and directors interested in furthering their understanding of film."[12] In 2003, he and his wife, Kate Capshaw, bought eight acres of land in Brentwood, California, to save it from commercial development. It was given to the Sullivan Canyon Preservation Association so residents can continue to exercise their horses there. In 1999, Spielberg received the first David Yurman Humanitarian Award. The award is a bronze sculpture of an angel and was given to the director as recognition of his work in the arts and his contributions to society. The award was presented at the GQ *Magazine* Men of the Year Awards in New York. The sculpture's designer, David Yurman, designs such awards to raise money for charities, and then he and his wife donate a portion of their proceeds back to charities. To help with the recovery in New Orleans after Hurricane Katrina hit there in 2005, Spielberg donated $1.5 million. He gave the same amount to help those suffering from the tsunami that hit Indonesia in December 2004. The philanthropic ventures of which he is most proud are offshoots of *Schindler's List:* The Shoah Foundation (see chapter 5) and the Righteous Persons Foundation. The second one is funded by receipts from the movie, and so far $37 million has gone to Holocaust and Jewish-community projects.

When a much younger Spielberg met Steven J. Ross, a former chairman of Time Warner, Ross became a father figure and remained so until his death in 1992. Before meeting him, Spielberg had made donations, but always with his name attached. Ross showed him that it was more gratifying to give without recognition. He got the same message from his rabbi, who told him that giving to get recognition "goes unrecognized by God."[13] Ever since, Spielberg still gives, but wants recognition only if it will help the charity get more contributions. One such charity is Starlight Starbright Children's Foundation, of which he is Foundation Chairman Emeritus. Formerly two separate foundations, the two merged in July 2004. Spielberg was a co-founder of the Starbright Foundation and in 2005 was recognized for his "tremendous impact on the lives of seriously ill children and their families."[14] The foundation is all about helping seriously ill children and their families "through imaginative programs that educate, uplift their spirits, foster a sense of community and help alleviate the pain and fear of prolonged illness."[15] The 2005 dinner and auction raised $1.5 million. Spielberg has gotten other big names, such as Norman Schwarzkopf and Troy Aikman, to invest time and money in this organization. Regarding Starbright's work, Spielberg says, "It's not just about entertainment; it's unleashing the power of entertainment and emerging technologies to develop new tools to help these kids heal!"[16] In May 2006, *Forbes* announced its list of the most generous celebrities. Spielberg, Oprah Winfrey, and Angelina Jolie topped the list.

FUTURE PROJECTS

In June 2005, *Newsweek* writer Sean Smith asked Spielberg about retiring. Spielberg replied, "I've often asked myself that question, and my answer comes back the same way every time: I love it. Being a moviemaker means you get to live many, many lifetimes. It's the same reason audiences go to movies, I think. When my daughter Sasha was 5 years old, we would be watching something on TV and she'd point to a character on screen and say, 'Daddy, that's me.' Ten minutes later a new character would come on screen and she'd say, 'No, Daddy. That's me.' Throughout the movie she would pick different people to become. I think that's what we all do. We just don't say it as sweetly."[17] Several years before that he had said that he felt "driven to work on the projects that I want to work on. . . . The minute I feel I have achieved my goals, then I'll probably stop. But I don't know what my goals are. And I just love the work too much to lay back on the laurels that other people bestow on me. . . . There are a lot of different things I haven't done yet."[18]

And he appears to be doing them now. In Spring 2006, rumors were going around that the director was taking a year off, yet within months announcements came out that he is going into reality television with *The Apprentice* producer Mark Burnett. Spielberg has always felt a duty and desire to help new talent and says that this show will give him a chance to do more. *On the Lot* will narrow down a nationwide search to 16 contestants. The 16 will be divided into two teams and each team will produce a short movie in a designated genre each week with one person working as director. The contestants will have professional writers, actors, and crew available to them. Judges will be a studio audience and a panel that will include a movie executive and a film critic plus a weekly guest. The judges will view the films and the audience will vote. The film receiving the fewest votes will lose that week, and its director will be eliminated from the program. Not only will the winner meet Steven Spielberg, he/she will get his/her own office on the DreamWorks studio lot and a development deal. The show will be produced by Mark Burnett Productions, DreamWorks Television, and Amblin Television.

Spielberg is also getting more involved in computer games, trying them out and tweaking them. When he was shown a game that was a spin-off from *Jurassic Park* and *The Lost World*, he told the designers not to make it too bloody because it will bother the parents. But since he hates to leave anyone with hurt feelings, he praised them for their work on one of the dinosaurs. The game is based on his animated production, *Small Soldiers*, and the related toys are doing well at the cash registers although the film did not. In October 2005, Spielberg announced that he was teaming with the Los Angeles office of Electronic Arts, Inc. (EALA) to develop three games. (Electronic Arts is the offshoot of the DreamWorks Interactive studio that was sold to Electronic Arts in 2000.) "Having watched the game industry grow from a niche into a major creative force in entertainment," says Spielberg, "I have a great deal of respect for EA's understanding of the interactive format."[19] In March, 2006, the Gamasutra Web site announced that the first of the games will have a World War II/ British Special Operations Executive (SOE) theme. EALA's vice president and general manager, Neil Young, says that their relationship with Spielberg is "focused exclusively on producing original, new intellectual property."[20] Spielberg keeps an office at EALA and is there every week. "The thing that's wonderful about him," says Young, "is that he's almost egoless. He's clearly reached the point where he just doesn't need to do anything other than just contribute creatively"[21]

Spielberg also worked with Pinnacle Systems, Inc., and the LEGO Company to design the LEGO & Steven Spielberg MovieMaker Set, which lets children bring their LEGO designs to life. The set includes a PC Movie Camera, props, more than 400 LEGO pieces, and a book of movie-making tips. According to the article released by the PR newswire in November 2000, there are also guidance notes from Spielberg himself. The product became available in U.S. stores November 1, 2000, and worldwide in April 2001. In 2000, the product received the Best Interactive Children's Award and the Best Interactive Learning Award from the British Academy of Film and Television Arts Interactive Entertainment Awards.

In April 2006, it was announced that Spielberg and director Zhang Yimou will co-design the opening and closing ceremonies for the 2008 Beijing Olympics.

Spielberg is also one of the names behind the animated summer 2006 hit, *Monster House*. He is also working with Doris Kearns Goodwin on a project about Abraham Lincoln that will star Liam Neeson; and he is producing *Transformers*, a much-anticipated movie to come out the summer of 2007. He is also producing Clint Eastwood's next movies, *Red Sun, Black Sand* (aka *Letters from Iwo Jima*) and *Flags of Our Fathers*. *Red Sun, Black Sand* is described as "the Japanese companion piece"[22] to *Flags of Our Fathers*. It will be shot entirely in Japanese.

As for the long-awaited *Indiana Jones* and *Jurassic Park* sequels, they are both in the pre-production stages as of fall 2006. Harrison Ford *will* star as the aging Indy and has suggested that Virginia Madsen be his leading lady. Otherwise, there are rumors galore: Sean Connery will return as Indy's father; Natalie Portman will play Indy's daughter; and previous Indy heroines, Karen Allen and Kate Capshaw, will have cameos. Spielberg *will* direct and George Lucas and Frank Marshall *will* produce. As for *Jurassic Park IV*, since it is expected to be in production at the same time as the Indy movie, Spielberg will likely be producer only.

ACCLAIM

"What separates Spielberg from lesser directors," writes Cindy White for scifi.com, "is the attention to detail."[23] Spielberg has "directed, produced, or executive produced seven of the thirty top-grossing films of all time . . ."[24] writes the *Broadway World News Desk*. He has received the Fellowship of the Academy Award from the British, an award previously given only to Alfred Hitchcock, Charlie Chaplin, and David Lean. In 1995, he was honored by AFI with the Life Achievement Award. Their tribute address reads in part, "The youngest recipient of this award, Spielberg is one of the finest talents of his generation and the most commercially successful filmmaker in the history of the cinema."[25] Also in 1995, he received the John Huston Artists Rights Award for contributions to artists' rights and his work to prevent film alteration. He topped Alfred Hitchcock in 1999, when an *Entertainment Weekly* poll named him the best director of the twentieth century. In 2001, he was made a Knight of the Order of the British Empire (KBE) by the Queen for his contribution to the British film industry. In November of that year, he accepted the 10th Annual Britannia Award from the British Academy of Film & Television Arts in Los Angeles (BAFTA L.A.). Since the award was renamed the Stanley Kubrick Britannia for Excellence in Film that year, BAFTA. LA wanted Spielberg to be its first recipient. He received the award from Prince Andrew, the Duke of York. In June 2005, he was voted "cinema's greatest director"[26] by the readers of Britain's *Empire* magazine. This put him one notch above the British-born Hitchcock. In his biography of the director, John Baxter writes, "His mastery of cinema technology . . . is innate and effortless, his innocent flair and enjoyment disguising the complexities of what he knows."[27] When he accepted the Gold Hugo Award from his pal, Tom Cruise, on July 15, 2006, Spielberg said, "Every time I go to something like this, it really reminds me that I haven't made my *Lawrence of Arabia* yet—I haven't made my *Grapes of Wrath* yet. It makes me hungry. I will go home from this with a healthy appetite to keep working."[28] Considering the movies that Steven Spielberg has made, it is hard to imagine that the best may still be to come.

NOTES

1. International Movie Database, "Biography for Steven Spielberg," www.imdb.com (accessed Sept 22, 2005).

2. BBC News, "Spielberg honoured at Rome Awards," April 15, 2004, www.newsvote.bbc.co.uk.

3. Hollywood.com, "Spielberg to Receive Lifetime Achievement Award," May 10, 2006, www.hollywood.com.

4. WorldScreen.com, "Spielberg to Receive International Emmy Founders Award," New York, April 24, 2006, www.worldscreen.com.

5. Dominic Wills, "Steven Spielberg Biography," December 15, 2005, www.tiscali.co.uk.

6. Thane Peterson, "Hybrid Heaven in a Lexus," *Business Week* Online Reviews, March 8, 2006, www.businessweek.com.

7. Lawrence Toppman, "Nature will take film fest by storm," *Charlotte Observer,* April 2, 2006, www.thestate.com.

8. Quoted in Christopher Rocchio, "Pursuing a dream: City native founded SurDeis Film Festival," *Daily News Tribune,* April 4, 2006, www.dailynewstribune.com.

9. Quote in Frank Sanello, *Spielberg: The Man, The Movies, The Mythology* (Dallas: Taylor, 1996), 173.

10. Quote in Sanello, 175.

11. Derrick Feldmann, "Steven Spielberg," Graduate paper. The Center on Philanthopy at Indiana University, 2005.

12. Feldmann.

13. Quoted in Stephen J. Dubner, "Steven the Good," *The New York Times Magazine,* February 14, 1999, reprinted in *Steven Spielberg Interviews,* Lester D. Friedman and Brent Notbohm, eds. (Jackson: University Press of Mississippi, 2000), 234.

14. CSR Wire, "Starlight Starbright Children's Foundation Announces Gala Event Honoring Chairman Emeritus Steven Spielberg, March 17, 2005, www.csrwire.com.

15. Ibid.

16. Quoted in Feldmann.

17. Quoted in Sean Smith, "The King of the World: Spielberg talks about movies, terror and wonder, and why the *Oprah* thing bothered him—but only a little," *Newsweek*, June 27, 2005, 58, www.infotrac.galegroup.com/.

18. Quoted in Peter Biskind, "A World Apart," *Premiere*, May 1997, reprinted in *Steven Spielberg Interviews*, Lester D. Friedman and Brent Notbohm, eds. (Jackson: University Press of Mississippi, 2000), 205.

19. Quoted in Etonline.com, "Steven Spielberg's Got Game," October 14, 2005, www.et.tv.yahoo.com/.

20. Quoted in Brandon Sheffield, "EALA's Neil Young on Emotion, IP, and Overtime," Gamasutra Features, May 22, 2006, www.gamasutra.com/.

21. Quoted in Sheffield.

22. Quoted in Stax, "Ra's Seeing *Red*: Watanabe, Clint team up," IGN Film Force. March 10, 2006, www.filmforce.ign.com/articles.

23. Cindy White, "Review of *Minority Report*," www.scifi.com/.

24. BWW News Desk, "Steven Spielberg to Remake Mary Poppins Film?" www.broadwayworld.com/.

25. American Film Institute, "Steven Spielberg: Life Achievement Award 1995 Tribute Address," 1995, www.afi.com/, accessed April 4, 2006.

26. UPI News Track, "Spielberg voted top director," United Press International, June 2, 2005, www.infotrac.galegroup.com/.

27. John Baxter, *Steven Spielberg, The Unauthorised Biography* (London: HarperCollins, 1996), 7.

28. Quoted in Stephen M. Silverman, "Tom Cruise Surprises Steven Spielberg," July 17, 2006, www.people.aol.com/.

APPENDIX A

FILMS DIRECTED BY STEVEN SPIELBERG

1. *Interstellar* (projected 2009)
2. *Team of Rivals* (aka *Lincoln Biopic*) (projected 2008)
3. *Indiana Jones 4* (projected 2008)
4. *Munich* (2005)
5. *War of the Worlds* (2005)
6. *The Terminal* (2004)
7. *Catch Me If You Can* (2002)
8. *Minority Report* (2002)
9. *A.I. Artificial Intelligence* (2001)
10. *The Unfinished Journey* (1999)
11. *Saving Private Ryan* (1998)
12. *Amistad* (1997)
13. *The Lost World Jurassic Park* (1997)
14. *Steven Spielberg's Director's Chair* (1996) (VG)
15. *Schindler's List* (1993)
16. *Jurassic Park* (1993)
17. *Amazing Stories: Book One* (1992) (V) (segment "The Mission")
18. *Hook* (1991)
19. *The Visionary* (1990) (V) (segment "Par for the Course")
20. *Always* (1989)
21. *Indiana Jones and the Last Crusade* (1989)
22. *Empire of the Sun* (1987)

23. *The Color Purple* (1985)
24. *Amazing Stories*
    "The Mission" (1985) TV Episode
    "Ghost Train" (1985) TV Episode
25. *Indiana Jones and the Temple of Doom* (1984)
26. *Twilight Zone The Movie* (1983) (segment 2)
27. *E.T. the Extra-Terrestrial* (1982)
28. *Raiders of the Lost Ark* (1981)
29. *1941* (1979)
30. *Close Encounters of the Third Kind* (1977)
31. *Jaws* (1975)
32. *The Sugarland Express* (1974)
33. *Savage* (1973) (TV)
34. *Something Evil* (1972) (TV)
35. *Duel* (1971) (TV)
36. *Owen Marshall: Counselor at Law*
    "Eulogy for a Wide Receiver" (1971) TV Episode
37. *Columbo: Murder by the Book* (1971) (TV)
38. *The Psychiatrist*
    "Par for the Course" (1971) TV Episode
    "The Private World of Martin Dalton" (1971) TV Episode
39. *The Name of the Game*
    "Los Angeles 2017" (1971) TV Episode
40. *Night Gallery*
    "Make Me Laugh" (1971) TV Episode
41. *Marcus Welby, M.D.*
    "The Daredevil Gesture" (1970) TV Episode
42. *Night Gallery* (1969) (TV) (segment "Eyes")
43. *Amblin'* (1968)
44. *Firelight* (1964)
45. *Escape to Nowhere* (1962)
46. *Fighter Squad* (1960)
47. *The Last Gun* (1958)

Source: www.imdb.com, "Steven Spielberg," accessed December 6, 2006.

APPENDIX B

FILMS PRODUCED BY STEVEN SPIELBERG

There are many films produced by the Amblin and DreamWorks SKG studios that were not *personally* produced by Mr. Spielberg. They are not listed here.

There are also Spielberg-produced episodes of the animated programs that are not listed here.

1. *The Talisman* (executive producer)
2. *Interstellar* (producer) (projected 2009)
3. *Disturbia* (2007) (executive producer)
4. *The Pacific War* (mini) TV Series (executive producer)
5. *Jurassic Park IV* (pre-production) (executive producer)
6. *Nine Lives* (2007) (mini) TV Series (executive producer)
7. *On the Lot* (2007) TV Series (executive producer)
8. *When Worlds Collide* (2008) (producer)
9. *Team of Rivals* (aka *Lincoln Biopic*) (projected 2008) (producer)
10. *Transformers* (2007) (executive producer)
11. *Flags of Our Fathers* (2006) (producer)
12. *Letters from Iwo Jima* (aka *Red Sun, Black Sand*) (2006) (producer)
13. *Spell Your Name* (2006) (executive producer)
14. *Monster House* (2006) (executive producer)
15. *Munich* (2005) (producer)
16. *Memoirs of a Geisha* (2005) (producer)
17. *The Legend of Zorro* (2005) (executive producer)

18. *Into the West* (2005) (mini) TV Series (executive producer)
19. *The Terminal* (2004) (producer)
20. *Voices from the List* (2004) (V) (executive producer)
21. *Catch Me If You Can* (2002) (producer)
22. *Taken* (2002/I) (mini) TV Series (executive producer)
23. *Men in Black II* (2002) (executive producer)
24. *Band of Brothers* (2001) (mini) TV Series (executive producer)
25. *Jurassic Park III* (2001) (executive producer)
26. *A.I. Artificial Intelligence* (2001) (producer)
27. *Saving Private Ryan* (1998) (producer)
28. *The Mask of Zorro* (1998) (executive producer)
29. *Deep Impact* (1998) (executive producer)
30. *Amistad* (1997) (producer)
31. *Men in Black* (1997) (executive producer)
32. *The Lost Children of Berlin* (1997) (executive producer)
33. *Twister* (1996) (executive producer)
34. *Survivors of the Holocaust* (1996) (TV) (executive producer)
35. *Balto* (1995) (executive producer)
36. *Pinky and the Brain* (1995) TV Series (executive producer)
37. *Tiny Toon Adventures: Night Ghoulery* (1995) (TV) (executive producer)
38. *Casper* (1995) (executive producer)
39. *A Pinky & the Brain Christmas Special* (1995) (TV) (executive producer)
40. *ER* (1994) TV Series (executive producer) (1994)
41. *The Flintstones* (1994) (executive producer) (as Steven Spielrock)
42. "I'm Mad!" (1994) (executive producer) (*Animaniacs* short feature)
43. "Tiny Toon Adventures: Spring Break Special" (1994) (TV) (executive producer)
44. "Tiny Toons Spring Break" (1994) (TV) (executive producer)
45. "Yakko's World: An Animaniacs Singalong" (1994) (V) (executive producer)
46. *SeaQuest DSV* (1993) TV Series (executive producer) (1993–1995)
47. *Schindler's List* (1993) (producer)
48. *We're Back! A Dinosaur's Story* (1993) (executive producer)
49. *Animaniacs* (1993) TV Series (executive producer)
50. *Class of '61* (1993) (TV) (executive producer)
51. *SeaQuest DSV* (1993) (TV) (executive producer)

52. "It's a Wonderful Tiny Toons Christmas Special" (1992) (TV) (executive producer)
53. "Tiny Toon Adventures: How I Spent My Vacation" (1992) (V) (executive producer)
54. *An American Tail: Fievel Goes West* (1991) (producer)
55. *Tiny Toon Adventures* (1990) TV Series (executive producer)
56. *Arachnophobia* (1990) (executive producer)
57. *Gremlins 2: The New Batch* (1990) (executive producer)
58. *Back to the Future Part III* (1990) (executive producer)
59. *Joe Versus the Volcano* (1990) (executive producer)
60. *Always* (1989) (producer)
61. *Back to the Future Part II* (1989) (executive producer)
62. *Dad* (1989) (executive producer)
63. *The Land Before Time* (1988) (executive producer)
64. *Who Framed Roger Rabbit* (1988) (executive producer)
65. **batteries not included* (1987) (executive producer)
66. *Empire of the Sun* (1987) (producer)
67. *Innerspace* (1987) (executive producer)
68. *Amazing Stories* (executive producer)
69. *An American Tail* (1986) (executive producer)
70. *The Money Pit* (1986) (executive producer)
71. *Young Sherlock Holmes* (1985) (executive producer)
72. *Back to the Future* (1985) (executive producer)
73. *The Goonies* (1985) (executive producer)
74. *Gremlins* (1984) (executive producer)
75. *Twilight Zone The Movie* (1983) (producer)
76. *Poltergeist* (1982) (producer)
77. *E.T. the Extra-Terrestrial* (1982) (producer)
78. *Continental Divide* (1981) (executive producer)
79. *Used Cars* (1980) (executive producer)
80. *I Wanna Hold Your Hand* (1978) (executive producer)

APPENDIX C

AWARDS

1962 Arizona Amateur Film Festival, First Prize, *Escape to Nowhere*

1973 Avoriaz (France) Fantastic Film Festival, Grand Prize, *Duel* (1971) (TV)

1974 Cannes Film Festival, Best Screenplay, *The Sugarland Express* (1974) (Shared with Hal Barwood & Matthew Robbins)

1978 Academy of Science Fiction, Fantasy & Horror Films, USA, Saturn Award, Best Director, *Close Encounters of the Third Kind* (1977) (Tied with George Lucas *Star Wars* [1977])

1982 ShoWest Convention, USA, Director of the Year

1982 Los Angeles Film Critics Association Awards (LAFCA), Best Director, *E.T. the Extra-Terrestrial* (1982)

1982 Saturn, Best Director, *Raiders of the Lost Ark* (1981)

1982 American Movie Awards' Marquee Award, Best Director, *Raiders of the Lost Ark* (1981)

1982 Kinema Junpo Awards, Readers' Choice Award, Best Foreign Language Film, *Raiders of the Lost Ark* (1981)

1982 Boston Society of Film Critics Awards (BSFC), Best Director, *Raiders of the Lost Ark* (1981)

1983 Boston Society of Film Critics Awards (BSFC), Best Director, *E.T. the Extra-Terrestrial* (1982)

1983 National Society of Film Critics Awards, USA (NSFC), Best Director, *E.T. the Extra-Terrestrial* (1982)

1983   Kinema Junpo Awards, Best Foreign Language Film, *E.T. the Extra-Terrestrial* (1982)

1983   Kinema Junpo Awards, Readers' Choice Award, Best Foreign Language Film, *E.T. the Extra Terrestrial* (1982)

1983   France's Cesar Awards' Honorary Cesar

1983   Harvard University's Hasty Pudding Theatricals, USA, Man of the Year

1983   David di Donatello Awards (Italy), David, Best Director of a Foreign Film, *E.T. the Extra-Terrestrial* (1982)

1983   Kansas City Film Critics Circle (KCFCC), Best Director, *E.T. the Extra-Terrestrial* (1982)

1983   Fotogramas de Plata Best (Spain), Foreign Film, *E.T. the Extra-Terrestrial* (1982)

1983   Blue Ribbon Award (Japan), Best Foreign Language Film, *E.T. the Extra-Terrestrial* (1982)

1984   Giffoni Film Festival (Italy), Nocciola d'Oro Award

1986   Directors Guild of America, USA Award (DGA), Outstanding Directorial Achievement in Motion Pictures, *The Color Purple* (1985) (Shared with Gerald R. Molen, unit production manager; Pat Kehoe, first assistant director; Richard A. Wells, first assistant director; Victoria E. Rhodes, second assistant director.)

1986   British Academy of Film and Television Arts Awards (BAFTA) Academy Fellowship

1986   Kansas City Film Critics Circle (KCFCC) Award, Best Director, *The Color Purple* (1985)

1987   Blue Ribbon Award (Japan), Best Foreign Language Film, *The Color Purple* (1985)

1987   National Board of Review, USA Award (NBR), Best Director, *Empire of the Sun* (1987)

1987   The Academy of Motion Picture Arts and Sciences (Academy Awards), Irving G. Thalberg Memorial Award

1988   Kansas City Film Critics Circle Award (KCFCC), Best Director, *Empire of the Sun* (1987)

1989   American Cinematheque Award (California)

1990   Retirement Research Foundation, USA, Wise Owl Award, Television and Theatrical Film Fiction, *Dad* (1989) (Shared with Gary David Goldberg, Joseph Stern, Kathleen Kennedy, Frank Marshall)

1990   American Cinema Editors, USA, Golden Eddie, Filmmaker of the Year Award

1991   Daytime Emmy, Outstanding Animated Program, *Tiny Toon Adventures* (1990) (Shared with Tom Ruegger, senior producer; Ken Boyer, director; Art Leonardi, director; Art Vitello, director; Paul Dini, story editor; Sherri Stoner, writer)

1993   Venice Film Festival, Career Golden Lion

1993   Boston Society of Film Critics Awards (BSFC), Best Director, *Schindler's List* (1993)

1993   Daytime Emmy, Outstanding Animated Program, *Tiny Toon Adventures* (1990) (Shared with Tom Ruegger, senior producer; Sherri Stoner, writer; Rich Arons, director; Byron Vaughns, director; Ken Boyer, director; Alfred Gimeno, director; David West, director)

1994   The Academy of Motion Picture Arts and Sciences (Academy Awards), Best Director Oscar, *Schindler's List* (1993)

1994   The Academy of Motion Picture Arts and Sciences (Academy Awards), Best Picture Oscar *Schindler's List* (1993) (Shared with Gerald R. Molen & Branko Lustig)

1994   Kansas City Film Critics Circle Award (KCFCC), Best Director, *Schindler's List* (1993)

1994   Hochi Film Awards (Japan), Best Foreign Language Film, *Schindler's List* (1993)

1994   Dallas-Fort Worth Film Critics Association Awards (DFWFCA), Best Director, *Schindler's List* (1993)

1994   Chicago Film Critics Association Awards (CFCA), Best Director, *Schindler's List* (1993)

1994   Amanda Awards (Norway), Best Foreign Feature Film, *Schindler's List* (1993)

1994   Czech Lions, Best Foreign Language Film, *Jurassic Park* (1993)

1994   Mainichi (Japan) Film Concours, Reader's Choice Award, Best Foreign Language Film, *Jurassic Park* (1993)

1994   Directors Guild of America, USA (DGA), Outstanding Directorial Achievement in Motion Pictures, *Schindler's List* (1993) (Shared with Branko Lustig, unit production manager; Sergio Mimica-Gezzan, first assistant director; Michael Helfand, second assistant director)

1994   The National Society of Film Critics Awards, USA (NSFC), Best Director, *Schindler's List* (1993)

1994   Academy of Science Fiction, Fantasy & Horror Films, USA, Saturn Award, Best Director, *Jurassic Park* (1993)

1994   Academy of Science Fiction, Fantasy & Horror Films, USA, Saturn Award, President's Award

1994   British Academy of Film and Television Arts Awards (BAFTA), Best Film, *Schindler's List* (1993) (Shared with Gerald R. Molen & Branko Lustig)

1994   British Academy of Film and Television Arts Awards (BAFTA), David Lean Award, Direction, *Schindler's List* (1993)

1994   Blue Ribbon Award (Japan), Best Foreign Language Film, *Jurassic Park* (1993)

1994   American Society of Cinematographers, USA, Board of the Governors Award

1994   Producers Guild of America (PGA), Motion Picture Producer of the Year, *Schindler's List* (1993) (Shared with Branko Lustig & Gerald R. Molen)

1994   Young Artist Awards, Jackie Coogan Award

1994   Golden Globes, Best Director of a Motion Picture, *Schindler's List* (1993)

1994   ShoWest Convention, USA, Director of the Year

1995   Society of Camera Operators, Governors Award

1995   American Film Institute, USA (AFI), Lifetime Achievement Award

1995   Mainichi Film Concours (Japan), Reader's Choice Award, Best Foreign Language Film, *Schindler's List* (1993)

1995   Kinema Junpo Awards (Japan), Reader's Choice Award, Best Foreign Language Film, *Schindler's List* (1993)

1995   London Critics Circle Film Awards (ALFS), Director of the Year, *Schindler's List* (1993)

1996   Daytime Emmy Awards, Outstanding Animated Program (Programming One Hour or Less), *A Pinky & the Brain Christmas Special* (1995) (TV) (Shared with Tom Ruegger, senior producer; Peter Hastings, producer/writer; Rusty Mills, producer/director)

1997   Daytime Emmy Awards, Outstanding Special Class Animated Program, *Freakazoid!* (1995) (Shared with Tom Ruegger, senior producer; Rich Arons, producer; John P. McCann, producer/writer; Paul Rugg, producer/writer; Mitch Schauer, producer; Ronaldo Del Carmen, director; Jack Heiter, director; Scott Jeralds, director; Eric Radomski, director; Dan Riba, director; Peter Shin, director)

1998   *Bundesverdienstkreuz mit Stern* (Federal Cross of Merit), Federal Republic of Germany

1998   Las Vegas Film Critics Society Awards, Sierra Award, Best Director, *Saving Private Ryan* (1998)(Tied with Roberto Benigni *Vita è bella, La* [1997])

1998   Toronto Film Critics Association Awards (TFCA), Best Director, *Saving Private Ryan* (1998)

1998   Producers Guild of America (PGA), Vision Award, *Amistad* (1997) (Shared with Debbie Allen & Colin Wilson)

1998   Rembrandt Awards (Netherlands), Audience Award, Best Director, *The Lost World Jurassic Park* (1997)

1999   Directors Guild of America, USA Award (DGA), Outstanding Directorial Achievement in Motion Pictures, *Saving Private Ryan* (1998) (Shared with Mark Huffam, production manager; Sergio Mimica-Gezzan, first assistant director; Adam Goodman, second assistant director; Karen Richards, second second assistant director)

1999   Distinguished Public Service Award, the U.S. Navy's highest civilian honor

1999   Italian National Syndicate of Film Journalists, Silver Ribbon, Best Director of a Foreign Film, *Saving Private Ryan* (1998)

1999   Daytime Emmy Awards, Outstanding Special Class Animated Program, *Pinky and the Brain* (1995) (Shared with Tom Ruegger, senior producer; Rusty Mills, supervising producer/director; Liz Holzman, producer/director; Charles M. Howell IV, producer/writer; Gordon Bressack, writer; Jed Spingarn, writer; Wendell Morris, writer; Tom Sheppard, writer; Earl Kress, writer; Andrea Romano, director; Russell Calabrese, director; Kirk Tingblad, director; Mike Milo, director; Nelson Recinos, director; Charles Visser, director)

1999   Daytime Emmy Awards, Outstanding Children's Animated Program, *Pinky, Elmyra & the Brain* (1998) (Shared with Tom Ruegger, senior producer; Rusty Mills, supervising producer/director; Liz Holzman, producer/director; Charles M. Howell IV, producer/writer; John P. McCann, producer/writer; Wendell Morris, writer; Tom Sheppard, writer; Gordon Bressack, writer; Douglas Langdale, writer; Kate Donahue, writer; Scott Kreamer, writer; Andrea Romano, director; Nelson Recinos, director; Russell Calabrese, director; Robert Davies, director)

1999   Online Film Critics Society Awards (OFCS), Best Director, *Saving Private Ryan* (1998)

1999   Producers Guild of America (PGA), Golden Laurel Awards, Motion Picture Producer of the Year, *Saving Private Ryan* (1998) (Shared with Allison Lyon Segan, Bonnie Curtis, Ian Bryce, Mark Gordon, and Gary Levinsohn)

1999   Producers Guild of America (PGA), Milestone Award

1999   Golden Globe, USA, Best Director of a Motion Picture, *Saving Private Ryan* (1998)

1999   Southeastern Film Critics Association Awards (SEFCA), Best Director, *Saving Private Ryan* (1998)

1999   Kansas City Film Critics Circle Award (KCFCC), Best Director, *Saving Private Ryan* (1998)

1999   UK's Empire Award, Best Director, *Saving Private Ryan* (1998)

1999   Czech Lions, Best Foreign Language Film, *Saving Private Ryan* (1998)

1999   The Academy of Motion Picture Arts and Sciences (Academy Awards), Best Director, *Saving Private Ryan* (1998)

1999   Best Director of the Twentieth Century, *Entertainment Weekly* poll

1999   Broadcast Film Critics Association Awards (BFCA), Best Director, *Saving Private Ryan* (1998)

2000   Directors Guild of America, USA, Lifetime Achievement Award

2000   Producers Guild of America (PGA), Hall of Fame—Motion Pictures, *E.T. the Extra-Terrestrial* (1982) (Shared with Kathleen Kennedy)

2000   NAACP Image Awards, Vanguard Award

2000   Daytime Emmy Awards, Outstanding Children's Animated Program, ~~Pinky, Elmyra & the Brain~~ (1998) (Shared with Tom Ruegger, senior producer; Rusty Mills, supervising producer; John P. McCann, producer/writer; Charles M. Howell IV, producer; Tom Sheppard, writer; Wendell Morris, writer; Gordon Bressack, writer; Earl Kress, writer; Andrea Romano, director; Robert Davies, director; Nelson Recinos, director)

2001   British Academy of Film and Television Arts Los Angeles (BAFTA LA), Britannia, Excellence in Film

2001   Venice Film Festival, Future Film Festival Digital Award, *A.I. Artificial Intelligence* (2001)

2001   Knight of the Order of the British Empire (KBE)

2001   National Board of Review, USA, Billy Wilder Award

2002   Producers Guild of America (PGA), Golden Laurel Awards, Television Producer of the Year in Longform, *Band of Brothers* (2001) (mini) (Shared with Tom Hanks & Tony To)

2002   Hollywood Film Festival Award, Best Feature Film, *Minority Report*

2002   Mainichi Film Concours (Japan), Reader's Choice Award, Best Foreign Language Film, *A.I. Artificial Intelligence* (2001)

2002   Academy of Science Fiction, Fantasy & Horror Films, USA, Saturn, Best Writing, *A.I. Artificial Intelligence* (2001)

2002   Christopher Awards, *Band of Brothers* (2001) (mini) (Shared with Phil Alden Robinson, director; Richard Loncraine, director; Mikael Salomon, director; David Nutter, director; Tom Hanks, director/writer/executive producer; David Leland, director; David Frankel, director; Tony To, director/co-executive producer; Erik Jendresen, writer; John Orloff, writer; E. Max Frye, writer; Graham Yost, writer; Bruce C. McKenna, writer; Erik Bork, writer; Mary Richards, producer; Stephen Ambrose, co-executive producer; Gary Goetzman, co-executive producer)

2002   ShoWest Convention, USA, Lifetime Achievement Award

2002   Yale University, Honorary Doctor of Humane Letters

2002   Daytime Emmy Awards, Outstanding Mini-series, *Band of Brothers* (2001) (mini), (Shared with Tom Hanks, executive producer; Stephen Ambrose, co-executive producer; Gary Goetzman, co-executive producer; Tony To, co-executive producer; Erik Bork, supervising producer; Erik Jendresen, supervising producer; Mary Richards, producer)

2003   Daytime Emmy Awards, Outstanding Mini-series, *Taken* (2002/ I) (mini) (Shared with Leslie Bohem, executive producer; Steve Beers, co-executive producer; Darryl Frank, co-executive producer; Joe M. Aguilar, co-executive producer; Richard Heus, producer)

2003   Academy of Science Fiction, Fantasy & Horror Films, USA, Saturn Award, Best Director, *Minority Report* (2002)

2003   *Empire* Awards (UK), Best Director, *Minority Report* (2002)

2003   Star on the Walk of Fame at 6801 Hollywood Blvd. on January 10, 2003

2003   Broadcast Film Critics Association Awards (BFCA), Best Director, *Catch Me If You Can (2002)* and *Minority Report* (2002)

2004   Tokyo International Film Festival, Akira Kurosawa Award

2004   Knight of the Legion of Honor of France

2004   David di Donatello Awards (Italy), Special David

2004   Cavaliere di Gran Croce, Italy

2005   Science Fiction Hall of Fame; Seattle, Washington, Inductee

2005   *Empire* Awards (UK), "Cinema's greatest director"

2005   Washington D.C. Area Film Critics Association Awards (WAFCA), Best Director, *Munich* (2005)

2006   Western Heritage Awards, Bronze Wrangler, Outstanding Television Feature Film, *Into the West* (2005) (mini) (Shared with Darryl Frank, producer; Justin Falvey, producer; David A. Rosemont, producer; William Mastrosimone, producer/writer; Kirk Ellis, producer/writer; Larry Rapaport, producer; Matthew Settle, actor;

Skeet Ulrich, actor; Tonantzin Carmelo, actor; Irene Bedard, actor; Michael Spears, actor; Zahn McClarnon, actor; Rachael Leigh Cook, actor)

2006   Chicago International Film Festival, Gold Hugo, Lifetime Achievement Award

2006   International Emmy Awards, International Emmy Founders Award British Academy of Film and Television Arts Awards (BAFTA), Academy Fellowship

2006   Art Directors Guild, Contribution to Cinematic Imagery

2006   Kansas City Film Critics Circle Awards (KCFCC), Best Director, *Munich* (2005)

2006   Kennedy Center of Performing Arts, Kennedy Center Honor.

APPENDIX D

TOP-GROSSING FILMS: ALL-TIME WORLDWIDE BOX-OFFICE RECORDS

RANK	TITLE AND YEAR RELEASED	GROSS DURING THEATRICAL RUN
6	*Jurassic Park*, 1993	919,700,000
20	*E.T. the Extra Terrestrial*, 1982	756,700,000
30	*Lost World Jurassic Park*, 1997	614,300,000
32	*War of the Worlds*, 2005	591,377,056
45	*Indiana Jones and the Last Crusade*, 1989	494,800,000
49	*Saving Private Ryan*, 1998	479,300,000
51	*Jaws*, 1975	470,600,000
83	*Raiders of the Lost Ark*, 1981	383,900,000
95	*Jurassic Park III*, 2001	362,900,000
100	*Minority Report*, 2002	358,000,000
122	*Catch Me If You Can*, 2002	337,400,000
126	*Indiana Jones and the Temple of Doom*, 1984	330,000,000
134	*Schindler's List*, 1993	321,200,000
150	*Hook*, 1991	300,800,000
154	*Close Encounters of the Third Kind*, 1977	300,000,000
239	*A.I. Artificial Intelligence*, 2001	230,000,000
259	*The Terminal*, 2004	217,845,279

Per International Movie Database, August 27, 2006, www.imdb.com.

The table above includes movies that have grossed over $200 million at the box office during their theatrical runs.

All amounts are in U.S. dollars and only include theatrical box office receipts (movie ticket sales) and do not include video rentals, television rights, and other revenues. Totals may include theatrical re-release receipts. Figures are not adjusted for inflation.

Note from the author: These are Steven Spielberg's movies only. To put these ratings in perspective, there were a total of 291 movies on the list.

APPENDIX E

CHARITABLE ORGANIZATIONS SUPPORTED BY SPIELBERG

USC Shoah Foundation
Steve Klappholz
Vice President for Development
USC Shoah Foundation
Institute for Visual History and Education
Leavey Library
650 W. 35th Street, Suite 114
Los Angeles, CA 90089-2571
(213) 740-6051
Fax: (213) 740-3896
vhi-web@usc.edu
http://www.usc.edu/schools/college/vhi/

Righteous Persons Foundation
Rachel Levin, Prog. Off.
2800 28th St., Ste. 105
Santa Monica, CA 90405
(310) 314-8393
Fax: (310) 314-8396
grants@righteouspersons.org
http://www.righteouspersons.org

Starlight Starbright Children's Foundation
5757 Wilshire Blvd, Suite M100
Los Angeles, CA 90036
(310) 479-1212
(800) 315-2580
Fax: (310) 479-1235
info@starlight.org
www.starlight.org

Cedars-Sinai Medical Center, West Hollywood
Steven Spielberg Pediatric Research Center
Steven Spielberg Building
8725 Alden Dr
Los Angeles, CA 90048
1-800-CEDARS-1 (1-800-233-2771)
Fax: (310) 423-4131
http://www.cmsc.edu/2675.html

Sullivan Canyon Preservation Association
321 South Beverly Drive, Suite M
Beverly Hills, CA 90212
(310) 454-5905
Fax: (310) 556-2924
info@access-scpa.org
http://www.access-scpa.org

The Planetary Society
65 North Catalina Avenue
Pasadena, CA 91106-2301
(626) 793-5100
Fax: (626) 793-5528
tps@planetary.org
(JavaScript required to read email)
http://planetary.org/home

University of Southern California
USC School of Cinema-Television
Attn: Production Program
University Park, LUC-404
Los Angeles, CA 90089-2211
(213) 740-3317
Fax: (213) 740-3395
productionoffice@cinema.usc.edu
http://cinemail.usc.edu

BIBLIOGRAPHY

AARP magazine. "The Fearless 50," March–April 2003. www.aarpmagazine.org.

Abagnale, Frank W. "Abagnale & Associates Comments." September 3, 2002. www.abagnale.com.

Abramowitz, Rachel. "*War* over, Spielberg moves on; As his blockbuster takes theaters, he's wrapped up in the aftermath of the '72 Munich killings." *Los Angeles Times*, July 1, 2005, E1. www.proquest.umi.com.

Adherents.com. "Religious Affiliation of Director Steven Spielberg." www.adherents.com (undated electronic work).

Adventures of Indiana Jones, The. Bonus Material. The Complete DVD Movie Collection. Four videodiscs. Directed by Steven Spielberg. Hollywood: Paramount Pictures/Lucasfilm Ltd., 2003, 1989, 1984, 1981.

American Film Institute. "Steven Spielberg: Life Achievement Award 1995 Tribute Address." www.afi.com (undated electronic work).

Andersen, Soren. "*War* wins some battles: Steven Spielberg's take on H.G. Wells' *War of the Worlds* is effectively scary but breaks no new ground." *News Tribune* (Tacoma, WA), July 1, 2005, South Sound edition, p. F24. www.proquest.umi.com.

Anderson, Lisa. "Fiennes Sits on the Brink of Major Stardom." *Chicago Tribune*. February 10, 1994. Reprinted in *Oskar Schindler and His List: The Man, the Book, the Film, the Holocaust and Its Survivors*. Thomas Fensch, ed., Introduction by Herbert Steinhouse. Forest Dale, VT: Paul S. Eriksson, 1995.

Ansen, David. "Spielberg's Obsession." *Newsweek*, December 20, 1993. Reprinted in *Oskar Schindler and His List: The Man, the Book, the Film, the Holocaust and Its Survivors*. Thomas Fensch, ed., Introduction by Herbert Steinhouse. Forest Dale, VT: Paul S. Eriksson, 1995.

Armstrong, Mark. "Spielberg's Knight Moves." *E! Online News*, December 28, 2000. www.eonline.com.

Ask.com. "Steven Spielberg." www.askmen.com (undated electronic work).

Au.Movies.Yahoo.com. "Steven Spielberg—Family and Companions." www.au.movies.yahoo.com (undated electronic work).

———. "Steven Spielberg—Milestones," July 5, 2006. www.au.movies.yahoo.com.

Awalt, Steven. Editor, lead writer, www.SpielbergFilms.com.

Bahiana, Ana Maria. "*Hook.*" *Cinema Papers*, March–April 1992. Reprinted in *Steven Spielberg Interviews*. Lester D. Friedman and Brent Notbohm, eds. Conversations with Filmmakers Series. Peter Burnette, general editor. Jackson: University Press of Mississippi, 2000.

Banerjee, Subhajit. "Now, music goes DTS, New Format Clarity." *Telegraph*, May 15, 2006. www.telegraphindia.com.

Baxter, John. *Mythmaker: Life and Work of George Lucas*. New York: Avon, 1999.

———. *Steven Spielberg, The Unauthorised Biography*. London: HarperCollins, 1996.

BBC News. "DreamWorks profits fall on costs," May 2, 2006. www.news.bbc.co.uk.

———. "Spielberg honoured at Rome awards," April 15, 2004. www.newsvote.bbc.co.uk.

———. "Spielberg series sued for haircut," March 18, 2006. www.newsvote.bbc.co.uk.

Bernstein, Fred A. "Steven Spielberg's Mother. An Interview with Leah Adler." *The Jewish Mothers' Hall of Fame*. New York: Doubleday, 1986. www.fredbernstein.com.

Billen, Andrew. "The True Drama of War." *New Statesman*, October 8, 2001, p. 46. www.web7.infotrac.galegroup.com.

Biskind, Peter. "A World Apart." *Premiere*, May 1997. Reprinted in *Steven Spielberg Interviews*. Lester D. Friedman and Brent Notbohm, eds. Conversations with Filmmakers Series. Peter Burnette, general editor. Jackson: University Press of Mississippi, 2000.

Bobrow, Andrew C. "Filming *The Sugarland Express*: An Interview with Steven Spielberg." *Filmmakers Newsletter*, Summer 1974. Reprinted in *Steven Spielberg Interviews*. Lester D. Friedman and Brent Notbohm, eds. Conversations with Filmmakers Series. Peter Burnette, general editor. Jackson: University Press of Mississippi, 2000.

Breznican, Anthony. "Family Relationships Fuel Spielberg's Films: Director Interview: *War of the Worlds*." *Seattle Times*, July 1, 2005, p. 120. www.proquest.umi.com.

———. "Spielberg's Family Values." *USA Today*, July 5, 2006. www.usatoday.com.

Brooks, Tim, and Earle Marsh, eds. "Amazing Stories." *Complete Directory to Prime Time Network and Cable TV Shows, 1946–Present,* 6th ed. New York: Ballantine Books, 1995, pp. 37–38.

Brown, Monica M. "HAFB Provides Sneak Peek of Film Location." *Alamagordo News,* May 21, 2006. www.alamogordonews.com.

Buckland, Warren. *Film Studies.* Series: Teach Yourself, 2nd ed. Chicago: McGraw-Hill, 2003.

BusinessWeek. "The Adventures of Steven Spielberg," July 13, 1998. www.businessweek.com.

———. "Anatomy of a Spielberg Hit," July 13, 1998. www.businessweek.com.

———. "Spielberg's Entertainment Empire," July 13, 1998. www.businessweek.com.

Business Wire. "Stars Align at the Science Fiction Museum and Hall of Fame," March 29, 2005. www.web2.infotrac.galegroup.com.

BWW News Desk. "Steven Spielberg to Remake Mary Poppins Film?" www.broadwayworld.com. Accessed March 1, 2006.

Byrne, Bridget. "Bill Gates Tops *Forbes* List of Richest Americans." E! Online News, September 29, 1997. www.eonline.com.

Carle, Chris. "*Transformers* Title Talk." IGN Film Force, May 23, 2006. www.filmforce.ign.com.

Carnegie Mellon University Department of Media Relations. "Carnegie Mellon University Announces 2006 Inductees into Robot Hall of Fame." April 19, 2006. www.roboticsonline.com.

Carpolipio, Redmond. "E3 revisited: Nintendo, Microsoft and Sony invite players into the next generation." U-Entertainment, May 18, 2006. www.dailynews.com.

Carter, Bill. "Shifting Arenas, Spielberg Joins Effort to make Reality TV Series." *The New York Times,* April 7, 2006. www.nytimes.com.

Catch Me If You Can: A Steven Spielberg Film. Introduction by Frank W. Abagnale. New York: Newmarket Pictorial Moviebook, Newmarket Press, 2002.

Catch Me If You Can. Bonus Features. *Catch Me If You Can,* DVD, directed by Steven Spielberg. Universal City, CA: DreamWorks Home Entertainment, 2002.

CBS News. "The Nominees: Steven Spielberg," February 28, 2006. www.cbsnews.com.

———. "Paramount to Buy DreamWorks," December 11, 2005. www.cbsnews.com.

Cedars-Sinai. "Steven Spielberg Pediatric Research Center." www.csmc.edu (undated electronic work).

CelebrityWonder. "Steven Spielberg Picture, Profile, Gossip, and News." www.celebritywonder.com (undated electronic work).

Champ, Zac. "The Steven Spielberg Directory." www.scruffles.net (undated electronic work).

Characters: The Family Unit. Special Features. *War of the Worlds,* DVD, directed by Steven Spielberg. Two-disc limited edition. Universal City, CA: DreamWorks Home Entertainment, 2005.

Chocano, Carina. "Movies: The Director's Art; To think like the masters; For Steven Spielberg, it takes a vicious alien attack to restore Dad as the head of the family." *Los Angeles Times,* July 10, 2005, p. E1. www.proquest.umi.com.

CNN.com. Steven Spielberg—Profile. "Hollywood's Master Storyteller." *People in the News.* www.cnn.com. Accessed July 5, 2006.

CNN.com. Steven Spielberg—Profile. "Steven Spielberg—Timeline." *People in the News.* www.cnn.com (undated electronic work).

———. "You Could Be the Next Steven Spielberg," April 7, 2006. www.cnn. worldnews.com.

Collaboration of Spirits, A: Casting and Acting The Color Purple. Bonus Features. *The Color Purple,* DVD, directed by Steven Spielberg. Burbank, CA: Warner Home Video, 2003.

Collins, Glenn. "Spielberg Films—*The Color Purple.*" *The New York Times,* December 15, 1985. Reprinted in *Steven Spielberg Interviews.* Lester D. Friedman and Brent Notbohm, eds. Conversations with Filmmakers Series. Peter Burnette, general editor. Jackson: University Press of Mississippi, 2000.

Color Purple, The: The Musical. Bonus Features. *The Color Purple,* DVD, directed by Steven Spielberg. Burbank, CA: Warner Home Video, 2003.

Combs, Richard. "Primal Scream." *Sight and Sound,* Spring 1977. Reprinted in *Steven Spielberg Interviews.* Lester D. Friedman and Brent Notbohm, eds. Conversations with Filmmakers Series. Peter Burnette, general editor. Jackson: University Press of Mississippi, 2000.

Contact Music. "Spielberg to Receive International Emmy," April 27, 2006. www.contactmusic.com.

Conversations with Ancestors: The Color Purple *from Book to Screen.* Bonus Features. *The Color Purple,* DVD, directed by Steven Spielberg. Burbank, CA: Warner Home Video, 2003.

Corliss, Richard. "No Artificial Intelligence: Just Smart Fun." *Time,* November 1, 2002. Reprinted in *Film Studies.* Warren Buckland, ed. Teach Yourself, 2nd ed. Series. Chicago: McGraw-Hill, 2003.

Corliss, Richard, and Jeffrey Ressner. "Peter Pan Grows Up: But Can He Still Fly?" *Time,* May 19, 1997, p. 74(9). Biography Resource Center. www. galenet.galegroup.com.

Cotsalas, Valerie. "The Hamptons' Most Coveted Spots." *The New York Times,* May 26, 2006. www.nytimes.com.

Cox, Dan. "Spielberg tapped for Huston Artists Rights Award." *Variety,* December 12, 1994, p. 27(1). www.find.galegroup.com.

Crawley, Tony. *The Steven Spielberg Story: The Man Behind the Movies.* New York: Quill, 1983.

CSRWire. "Starlight Starbright Children's Foundation Announces Gala Event Honoring Chairman Emeritus Steven Spielberg," March 17, 2005. www.csrwire.com.

Cuaycong, Anthony L. "Courtside." *BusinessWorld Manila*, July 1, 2005, p. 1. www.proquest.umi.com.

Daily Telegraph. "Invisible man." *Sydney Confidential*, May 26, 2006. www.dailytelegraph.com.au.

Davey, Ben, and Joanna Cohen. "Top five 'when animals attack' films." *Sydney Morning Herald*, April 6, 2006. www.smh.com.au.

Davidson, Paul. "Indy 4: Now or Never, Ford is Looking Forward to It." IGN Entertainment, January 23, 2006. www.filmforce.ign.com.

———. "Jurassic Park 4 Next Year, Writers Are Starting Over," April 19, 2006. www.filmforce.ign.com.

Davidson, Paul, and Stax. "Indy 4: Is There a Consensus? Ford and Lucas Say It's Ready to Go." IGN Entertainment, Inc., March 17, 2006. www.filmforce.ign.com/articles.

Davies, Hugh. "3-D can save Hollywood, says director," April 25, 2006. www.telegraph.co.uk.

Denby, David. "For the Love of Fighting." *New Yorker*, December 23, 2002, pp. 166–169. www.proquest.umi.com.

———. "Stayin' Alive." *New Yorker*, July 11, 2005, pp. 102. www.web2.infotrac.galegroup.com.

———. "Wanderers: The Current Cinema." *New Yorker*. July 5, 2004. pp. 99–101. www.proquest.umi.com.

DeWolfe, Anne, and Fred MacFarlane. "Starlight Children's Foundation and Starbright Foundation Merge; Newly-formed 'Starlight Starbright Children's Foundation' Makes Plans to 'Brighten the Lives of Seriously Ill Children' Worldwide," July 13, 2004. www.slsb.org.

Doherty, Thomas. "Schindler's List." *Cineaste* 20, no. 3 (1994). Reprinted in *Oskar Schindler and His List: The Man, the Book, the Film, the Holocaust and Its Survivors*. Thomas Fensch, ed., Introduction by Herbert Steinhouse. Forest Dale, VT: Paul S. Eriksson, 1995.

Downey, Margaret. "Spielberg Finally Convinced to Leave BSA." *Scouting for All*, July 2, 2001. www.scoutingforall.org.

Dubner, Stephen J. "Inside the Dream Factory." *Guardian Unlimited*, March 21, 1999. www.guardian.co.uk.

———. "Steven the Good." *The New York Times Magazine*. February 14, 1999. Reprinted in *Steven Spielberg Interviews*. Lester D. Friedman and Brent Notbohm, eds. Conversations with Filmmakers Series. Peter Burnette, general editor. Jackson: University Press of Mississippi, 2000.

Ebert, Roger. "*A.I. Artificial Intelligence*," June 29, 2001. www.rogerebert.suntimes.com.

———. "*Amistad.*" December 12, 1997. www.rogerebert.suntimes.com.

———. *The Great Movies II.* New York: Broadway Books, 2005.

———. "*The Lost World Jurassic Park,*" June 6, 1997. www.rogerebert.suntimes. com.

———. "*Minority Report.*" *Chicago Sun-Times* online, June 6, 2002. Reprinted in *Film Studies.* Warren Buckland ed., Teach Yourself, 2nd ed., Series. Chicago: McGraw-Hill, 2003.

———. "*Munich.*" December 23, 2005. www.rogerebert.suntimes.com.

———. "The *Time* 100." *Time:* The Most Important People of the Century, June 8, 1998. www.time.com.

Ejiofor, Mmoma. "Generous Celebs." *Forbes,* Lifestyle Feature, May 5, 2006. www.forbes.com.

Eller, Claudia. "GE Said to Have Okd Pursuit of Studio." *Los Angeles Times,* July 30, 2005, p. C1. www.proquest.umi.com.

Empire of the Sun. Special Features. DVD, directed by Steven Spielberg. Burbank, CA: Warner Home Video, 2001.

Erbach, Karen. "*Schindler's List* Finds Heroism Amidst Holocaust." *American Cinematographer,* January 1994. Reprinted in *Oskar Schindler and His List: The Man, the Book, the Film, the Holocaust and Its Survivors.* Thomas Fensch, ed., Introduction by Herbert Steinhouse. Forest Dale, VT: Paul S. Eriksson, 1995.

E.T. *Behind the Scenes. E.T. the Extra-Terrestrial,* Disc 2. DVD, directed by Steven Spielberg. Two-disc limited collector's edition. Widescreen version. Universal City, CA: Universal Home Video, 2002.

Etonline.com. "Steven Spielberg's Got Game." Etonline, October 14, 2005. www. et.tv.yahoo.com.

Farber, Stephen, and Marc Green. *Outrageous Conduct: Art, Ego, and the Twilight Zone Case.* New York: Ivy, 1989.

Fearon, Peter. *Hamptons Babylon: Life Among the Super-Rich on America's Riviera.* Secaucus, NJ: Birch Lane Press, Carol Publishing Group, 1998.

Feldmann, Derrick. "Steven Spielberg." Graduate Paper, The Center on Philanthropy at Indiana University, 2005.

Fensch, Thomas, ed. *Oskar Schindler and His List: The Man, the Book, the Film, the Holocaust and Its Survivors.* Introduction by Herbert Steinhouse. Forest Dale, VT: Paul S. Eriksson, 1995.

Fine, Marshall. "Amazon.com: *Duel* (Collector's Edition) DVD." www.amazon. com (undated electronic work).

Finn, Natalie. "Spielberg Gets Real for Fox." *E!* Online News, April 6, 2006. www.eonline.com.

Forbes. "*Forbes* Billionaires in Alphabetical Order." Associated Press, 2006. www. forbes.com/lists.

Forsberg, Myra. "Spielberg at 40: The Man and the Child." *The New York Times*, January 10, 1988. Reprinted in *Steven Spielberg Interviews*. Lester D. Friedman and Brent Notbohm, eds. Conversations with Filmmakers Series. Peter Burnette, general editor. Jackson: University Press of Mississippi, 2000.

Friedman, Lester D., and Brent Notbohm, eds. *Steven Spielberg Interviews*. Conversations with Filmmakers Series. Peter Burnette, general editor. Jackson: University Press of Mississippi, 2000.

Friedman, Roger. "Spielberg Will Take a Year Off." Fox411 News, March 6, 2006. www.foxnews.com/story.

GameSpot. "E3 06: CelebSpotting @ E3 06." www.gamespot.com (undated electronic work).

Gardner, David. *Tom Hanks: The Unauthorized Biography*. London: Blake, 1999.

Gawker.com. "Classic Gawker Stalker: Anna Wintour Suffers Through the Painfully Pedestrian Task of Jury Duty." www.gawker.com (undated electronic work).

Giles, Jeff. "Catch them if You Can: What do you want for Christmas? How about Spielberg behind the camera and Hanks and DiCaprio in front of it? A Candid Conversation." *Newsweek*, December 23, 2002, p. 58. www.web7.infotrac.galegroup.com.

Gleiberman, Owen. "The *E.T.* Effect." *Entertainment Weekly*, April 10, 2006. www.ew.com.

———. "Globe Trodders: The aliens are coming in Steven Spielberg's scary sci-fi spectacular, *War of the Worlds*. *Entertainment Weekly*, July 8, 2005, p. 45. www.web2.infotrac.galegroup.com.

———. Review of *Munich*. *Entertainment Weekly*, January 17, 2006. www.ew.com.

Glenn, Cheryl. "*Catch Me If You Can DVD* Features." February 26, 2003. www.web7.infotrac.galegroup.com. Accessed August 20, 2005.

Grossberg, Josh. "Ford: 'Indy 4' Script Ready," March 15, 2006. www.eonline.com.

———. "Oprah, Bono Top Celeb Philanthropists." E! Online News, May 11, 2006. www.eonline.com.

Grossman, Ben. "Fox Heads to Hollywood Lot." Broadcasting and Cable: The Business of Television, April 6, 2006. www.broadcastingcable.com.

Guthmann, Edward. "Spielberg's 'List': Director rediscovers his Jewishness while filming Nazi Story." *San Francisco Chronicle*, December 12, 1993. Reprinted in *Oskar Schindler and His List: The Man, the Book, the Film, the Holocaust and Its Survivors*. Thomas Fensch, ed., Introduction by Herbert Steinhouse. Forest Dale, VT: Paul S. Eriksson, 1995.

"H. G. *Wells Legacy*, The." Special Features. *War of the Worlds*, DVD, directed by Steven Spielberg. Two-disc limited edition. Universal City, CA: DreamWorks Home Entertainment, 2005.

Halbfinger, David M. "Next: Spielberg's Biggest Gamble." *The New York Times*, July 1, 2005, p. E 1. www.proquest.umi.com.

Hartl, John. "*Schindler's List*: A Commanding Holocaust Film." *Seattle Times*, December 15, 1993. Reprinted in *Oskar Schindler and His List: The Man, the Book, the Film, the Holocaust and Its Survivors*. Thomas Fensch, ed., Introduction by Herbert Steinhouse. Forest Dale, VT: Paul S. Eriksson, 1995.

Harvey, Fred. Review of *Amistad*. The History Place, December 20, 1997. www.historyplace.com.

Hearn, Marcus. *The Cinema of George Lucas*. Foreword by Ron Howard. New York: Harry N. Abrams, Inc., 2005.

HebrewSongs. "Oyfn Pripetchik." www.hebrewsongs.com (undated electronic work).

Helpern, David. "At Sea with Steven Spielberg." *Take One*, March–April 1974. Reprinted in *Steven Spielberg Interviews*. Conversations with Filmmakers Series. Lester D. Friedman and Brent Notbohm, eds. Peter Burnette, general editor. Jackson: University Press of Mississippi, 2000.

Hewitt, Chris. "Spielberg's *The Terminal*: Pay attention to the Nuts." *Saint Paul Pioneer Press* (via Knight-Ridder/Tribune News Service), June 14, 2004. www.web7.infotrac.galegroup.com.

Hibberd, James. "Unrest in the West: Some Native American extras allege they were mistreated during production of Steven Spielberg's epic miniseries *Into the West*, the largest project in TNT's history." TV Currents. *Television Week*, June 13, 2005, p. 1. www.web2.infotrac.galegroup.com.

Higgins, Bill. "Steven's list." (Steven Spielberg to receive honorary doctorate from University of Southern California). *Entertainment Weekly*, May 6, 1994, p. 11(1). www.find.galegroup.com.

Hirsch, Lisa. "Design kudos *Catch* hobbits (Art Directors Guild's Production Design Awards Banquet)." *Daily Variety*, February 24, 2003, p. 4(2). www.find.galegroup.com.

Hoberman, J. "Private Eyes." *Village Voice*, February 16, 2002. Reprinted in *Film Studies*. Warren Buckland, ed. Teach Yourself, 2nd ed., Series. Chicago: McGraw-Hill, 2003.

Hodenfield, Chris. "*1941*: Bombs Away." *Rolling Stone*, January 24, 1980. Reprinted in Lester D. Friedman and Brent Notbohm, eds. *Steven Spielberg Interviews*. Conversations with Filmmakers Series. Peter Burnette, general editor. Jackson: University Press of Mississippi, 2000.

Holden, Stephen. Review of *The Lost World: Jurassic Park*. *The New York Times*, May 23, 1997. www.nytimes.com.

Hollinger, Hy. "Family films battle World Cup for summer supremacy." Yahoo! News, April 25, 2006. www.news.yahoo.com.

Hollywood.com. "*Idol* Runner-Up Gets a Call From Spielberg," May 26, 2006. www.hollywood.com.

———. "Spielberg to Receive Lifetime Achievement Award," May 10, 2006. www.hollywood.com.

Hollywood Reporter. "More than 2,000 fans gathered June 3 for the inaugural *Jaws* Fest in Martha's Vineyard, Massachusetts. June 14, 2005, p. 16(1). www. web2.infotrac.galegroup.com.

Hull, Dana. "Pro-preschool campaign well ahead in fundraising." *Mercury News*, March 25, 2006. www.kansas.com.

I4U News. "Steven Spielberg and Shigeru Miyamoto Played Tennis on the Nintendo Wii." www.i4u.com (undated electronic work).

International Movie Database. "Amblin Entertainment." www.imdb.com (undated electronic work).

———. "Awards for *Close Encounters of the Third Kind.*" (1977) www.imdb.com (undated electronic work).

———. "Awards for *Jaws.*" (1975) www.imdb.com (undated electronic work).

———. "Awards for *Munich* ."(2005) www.imdb.com (undated electronic work).

———. "Awards for *The Sugarland Express.*" (1974) www.imdb.com (undate electronic work).

———. "Biography for Arnold Spielberg." www.imdb.com (undated electronic work).

———. "Biography for Steven Spielberg." www.imdb.com (undated electronic work).

———. "DreamWorks SKG." www.imdb.com (undated electronic work).

———. "Filmography for Steven Spielberg." www.imdb.com (undated electronic work).

———. "Max Spielberg." www.imdb.com (undated electronic work).

———. "Munich Terrorist Hits Out at Spielberg." Movie & TV News (undated electronic work).

———. "News for Arnold Spielberg," April 28, 2000. www.imdb.com (undated electronic work).

———. "Plot Summary for *Close Encounters of the Third Kind.*" (1977) www. imdb.com (undated electronic work).

———. "Plot Summary for *Jaws.*" (1975) www.imdb.com (undated electronic work).

———. "Plot Summary for *The Sugarland Express.*" (1974) www.imdb.com (un-dated electronic work).

———. "Spielberg 'Stunned' by Paramount's Cruise Decision," August 25, 2006. www.imdb.com.

———. "Spielberg's Son Follows in Footsteps," October 9, 2002. www.imdb.com.

————. "Trivia for *Close Encounters of the Third Kind*." (1977) www.imdb.com (undated electronic work).

————. "Trivia for *Jaws*." (1975) www.imdb.com (undated electronic work).

————. "Trivia for *Saving Private Ryan*." (1998) www.imdb.com (undated electronic work).

————. "Trivia for *The Sugarland Express*." (1974) www.imdb.com (undated electronic work).

James, Samuel. Review of *Saving Private Ryan*, May 27, 2006. Blogcritics.org. www.blogcritics.org.

Jenkins, David. "Report: EA's First Spielberg Collaboration Detailed." Gamasutra Report, March 24, 2006. www.gamasutra.com.

Kadlec, Daniel, and Jeffrey Ressner. "Three Moguls Aboard: After the *Shrek* wreck, who can right the DreamWorks ship?" *Time*, July 25, 2005, p. 49. www.web2.infotrac.galegroup.com.

Kauffmann, Stanley. *Saving Private Ryan*. New Republic, August 17, 1998, p. 24(1). www.web7.infotrac.galegroup.com.

————. "Spielberg Revisited." *New Republic*, January 24, 1994. Reprinted in *Oskar Schindler and His List: The Man, the Book, the Film, the Holocaust and Its Survivors*. Thomas Fensch, ed., Introduction by Herbert Steinhouse. Forest Dale, VT: Paul S. Eriksson, 1995.

Kelly, Kate and Merissa Marr. "DreamWorks SKG May Go to Universal." *Wall Street Journal* (Eastern Edition). New York: July 28, 2005, p. B.1. www.proquest.umi.com.

Kidsread.com. "*E.T. the Extra-Terrestrial's* 20th Anniversary." www.kidsread.com (undated electronic work).

King, Laura. "The Envelope: *Munich* seen more as a yawner than a winner." *Los Angeles Times*, March 1, 2006. www.calendarlive.com.

King, Thomas R. "Lucasvision." *Wall Street Journal*, 1994. Reprinted in *George Lucas Interviews*. Sally Kline, ed. Jackson: University of Mississippi, 1999.

King, Tom. *The Operator: David Geffen Builds, Buys, and Sells the New Hollywood*. New York: Random House, 2000.

Kline, Sally, ed. *George Lucas Interviews*. Jackson: University of Mississippi, 1999.

Kolker, Robert. *Film, Form, and Culture*. Boston: McGraw-Hill College, 1999.

Koltnow, Barry. "The Misfits: Hanks and Spielberg never fit in—which is why they're friends." *Orange County Register* (Santa Ana, CA) (via Knight-Ridder/Tribune News Service), June 16, 2004. www.web7.infotrac.galegroup.com.

Korte, Tim. "Spielberg Production Sued Over Haircut." Yahoo! News, March 17, 2006. www.news.yahoo.com.

Kozinn, Allan. "Philharmonic and Film: Sound to Bring Pictures to Life." *The New York Times*, April 26, 2006. www.nytimes.com.

Ladaw, Dennis. "The Hills Are Alive." Filmwatch. ABS-CBN Interactive. www.abs-cbnnews.com (undated electronic work).

Lee, Patrick. *A.I. Artificial Intelligence*. www.scifi.com. Accessed January 30, 2006.

"LEGO & Steven Spielberg MovieMaker Set Receives Prestigious Awards." *PR Newswire* (November 16, 2000): pNA. InfoTrac OneFile. Thomson Gale. August 14, 2006. www.find.galegroup.com.

Library of Congress. "Tribute to Mr. Arnold Spielberg." U.S. Senate, April 6, 2001. www.thomas.loc.gov.

Louvish, Simon. "Witness." *Sight and Sound*, March 1994. Reprinted in *Oskar Schindler and His List: The Man, the Book, the Film, the Holocaust and Its Survivors*. Thomas Fensch, ed., Introduction by Herbert Steinhouse. Forest Dale, VT: Paul S. Eriksson, 1995.

Macdonald, Moira. "*Munich*: A story of murder and unfathomable vengeance." *Seattle Times*, December 23, 2005. www.seattletimes.newsource.com.

Madatian, Jasmine. "Audiences March to *War*: Steven Spielberg–Tom Cruise Film Opens to $34.6 Million Worldwide in Its First Day." PR Newswire, June 30, 2005. www.web2.infotrac.galegroup.com.

Making of Close Encounters of the Third Kind, *The. Close Encounters of the Third Kind*, DVD, directed by Steven Spielberg. Collector's Edition. Culver City, CA: Columbia TriStar Home Entertainment, 2001.

Making *of* Jaws, *The. Jaws*, DVD, directed by Steven Spielberg. Anniversary Collector's Edition. Universal City, CA: Universal, 2000.

Making of Jurassic Park, *The. Jurassic Park*, DVD, directed by Steven Spielberg. Collector's Edition. Universal City, CA: Universal, 2000.

Making The Lost World Jurassic Park. *The Lost World Jurassic Park*, DVD, directed by Steven Spielberg. Collector's Edition. Universal City, CA: Universal, 2000.

Mansfield, Stephanie. "Liam Neeson Puts the Kettle On." *Vanity Fair*, December 1993. Reprinted in *Oskar Schindler and His List: The Man, the Book, the Film, the Holocaust and Its Survivors*. Thomas Fensch, ed., Introduction by Herbert Steinhouse. Forest Dale, VT: Paul S. Eriksson, 1995.

Maran, Meredith, and Anne McGrath, eds. *Amistad. 'give us free.' A Celebration of the Film by Steven Spielberg*. Essays by Maya Angelou, Debbie Allen. New York: Newmarket Press, 1998.

Maslin, Janet. Review of *Amistad*. Plot Description from Bhob Stewart, *All Movie Guide. The New York Times*. December 1997. www.nytimes.com.

Mattison, Ben. "Scorsese and Spielberg to Appear at New York Philharmonic's Evenings of Film Music." *Playbill Arts*, March 8, 2006. www.playbillarts.com.

McBride, Joseph. *"The Lost World: Jurassic Park."* Boxoffice Magazine. www.box-office.com (undated electronic work).

———. "A Portrait of the Artist as a Young Man." *BoxOffice* Online Cover Story. www.boxoffice.com (undated electronic work). Adapted by the author from Joseph McBride, *Steven Spielberg: A Biography.* New York: Simon and Schuster, 1997.

———. *Steven Spielberg: A Biography.* New York: Simon and Schuster, 1997.

McCarthy, Phillip. "The Trouble with Tom." *Sydney Morning Herald,* April 29, 2006. www.smh.com.au.

McCarthy, Todd. Review of *Minority Report.* www.variety.com. Reprinted in *Film Studies.* Warren Buckland, ed. Teach Yourself, 2nd ed., Series. Chicago: McGraw-Hill, 2003.

———. Review of *Saving Private Ryan. Variety,* July 20, 1998, p. 45(1). www.web7.infotrac.galegroup.com.

———. "Spielberg delivers thrills in *Worlds." Daily Variety,* June 29, 2005, p. 1(2). www.web2.infotrac.galegroup.com.

McCoy, Dave. Review of *Amistad* (1997). www.amazon.com (undated electronic work).

Menconi, David. "Universal delights: Check out the theme park in Orlando." *News and Observer,* April 23, 2006. www.newsobserver.com.

Menon, Shyam G. "War of the Worlds—A Great Spectacle." *Businessline,* Chennai, July 1, 2005, p. 1. www.proquest.umi.com.

Mikkelson, Barbara, and David P. Mikkelson. "The Universal Soldier." Urban Legends Reference Pages, November 18, 2003. www.snopes.com.

Miller, Lynda. "Hollywood Reporter Publishes Survey of Entertainment Industry Philanthropy." *The Hollywood Reporter,* July 24, 2002. www.pnnonline.org.

Minority Report Special Features. *Minority Report,* DVD, directed by Steven Spielberg. Universal City, CA: DreamWorks Home Entertainment, 2003.

Moran, Jonathon. "Australiana Jones." NEWS.com.au, April 4, 2006. www.entertainment.news.com.au.

Morgenstern, Joe. "Spielberg Comes Home; In Intense *War of the Worlds,* Family Values Trump Effects; Cruise and Dakota Fanning Anchor a Surprisingly Human Drama." *Wall Street Journal.* Weekend Journal. Eastern Edition, July 1, 2005, p. W1. www.proquest.com.

Munich Web site. "Commentaries." www.munichmovie.com. Accessed March 11, 2006.

Mystic in Ruins.com. "*Monster House* Trailer Comes to Life." Columbia Pictures, April 28, 2006. www.mysticinruins.com.

Parsons, Ryan. "Virginia Madsen Digs Indiana Jones," February 3, 2006. www.canmag.com.

People Weekly. "In Elite Ranks: Steven Spielberg and Tom Hanks get a Navy seal of approval for *Saving Private Ryan*," November 29, 1999, p. 90. www.find. galegroup.com.

———. Review of *Saving Private Ryan*. August 3, 1998, p. 25(1). www.web7. infotrac.galegroup.com.

Peterson, Thane. "Hybrid Heaven in a Lexus." *Business Week* Online Reviews, March 8, 2006. www.businessweek.com.

Pittam, Nicola. "Spielberg's Mom and the Milky Way," June 14, 2006. www.the-vu.com.

Pizzello, Stephen. "Five-Star General." *American Cinematographer*, August 1998. Reprinted in *Steven Spielberg Interviews*. Lester D. Friedman and Brent Notbohm, eds. Conversations with Filmmakers Series. Peter Burnette, general editor. Jackson: University Press of Mississippi, 2000.

Planetary Society. Board of Directors: Steven Spielberg. www.planetary.org.

Poster, Steve. "The Mind Behind *Close Encounters of the Third Kind*." *Cinematographer*, February 1978. Reprinted in *Steven Spielberg Interviews*. Lester D. Friedman and Brent Notbohm, eds. Conversations with Filmmakers Series. Peter Burnette, general editor. Jackson: University Press of Mississippi, 2000.

Pravda. "Cannes documentary *Boffo* explores Hollywood's hits and misses," May 25, 2006. www.english.pravda.ru.

PR Newswire. "*Catch Me If You Can* DVD Features," February 26, 2005. www. web7.infotrac.galegroup.com

———. "LEGO & Steven Spielberg MovieMaker Set Receives Prestigious Awards, November 16, 2000. www.find.galegroup.com.

Production Diaries: East Coast—Beginning. Special Features. *War of the Worlds*, DVD, directed by Steven Spielberg. Two-disc limited edition. Universal City, CA: DreamWorks Home Entertainment, 2005.

Production Diaries: East Coast—Exile. Special Features. *War of the Worlds*, DVD, directed by Steven Spielberg. Two-disc limited edition. Universal City, CA: DreamWorks Home Entertainment, 2005.

Production Diaries: West Coast—Destruction. Special Features. *War of the Worlds*, DVD, directed by Steven Spielberg. Two-disc limited edition. Universal City, CA: DreamWorks Home Entertainment, 2005.

Production Diaries: West Coast—War. Special Features. *War of the Worlds*, DVD, directed by Steven Spielberg. Two-disc limited edition. Universal City, CA: DreamWorks Home Entertainment, 2005.

Production Notes. Special Features. *War of the Worlds*, DVD, directed by Steven Spielberg. Two-disc limited edition. Universal City, CA: DreamWorks Home Entertainment, 2005.

Rafferty, Terrence. "A Man of Transactions." *New Yorker*, December 20, 1993. Reprinted in *Oskar Schindler and His List: The Man, the Book, the Film, the*

Holocaust and Its Survivors. Thomas Fensch, ed., Introduction by Herbert Steinhouse. Forest Dale, VT: Paul S. Eriksson, 1995.

Reunion, The: The Cast and Filmmakers Discuss the Impact of the Film. Disc 2. *E.T. the Extra-Terrestrial,* DVD, directed by Steven Spielberg. Two-disc limited collector's edition. Widescreen version. Universal City, CA: Universal Home Video, 2002.

Revisiting the Invasion. Special Features. *War of the Worlds,* DVD, directed by Steven Spielberg. Two-disc limited edition. Universal City, CA: DreamWorks Home Entertainment, 2005.

Richardson, John H. "Steven's Choice." *Premiere,* January 1994. Reprinted in *Steven Spielberg Interviews.* Lester D. Friedman and Brent Notbohm, eds. Conversations with Filmmakers Series. Peter Burnette, general editor. Jackson: University Press of Mississippi, 2000.

Roberts, Jerry, and Steven Gaydos. "10th annual Britannia Award from the British Academy of Film & Television Arts Los Angeles awarded to Steven Spielberg." *Variety,* October 30, 2000, p. 39. www.find.galegroup.com.

Roberts, Johnnie L. "Working the Dream: Now showing: DreamWorks' ambitious plan to rule the world of animated movies," *Newsweek,* May 16, 2005, p. 46. www.web2.infotrac.galegroup.com.

Rocchio, Christopher. "Pursuing a dream: City native founded SurDeis Film Festival." *Daily News Tribune,* April 4, 2006. www.dailynewstribune.com.

Rosenbaum, Jonathan. *Essential Cinema: On the Necessity of Film Canons.* Baltimore: Johns Hopkins University Press, 2004.

Royal, Susan. "*Always:* An Interview with Steven Spielberg." *American Premiere,* December–January 1989–90. Reprinted in *Steven Spielberg Interviews.* Lester D. Friedman and Brent Notbohm, eds. Conversations with Filmmakers Series. Peter Burnette, general editor. Jackson: University Press of Mississippi, 2000.

———. "Steven Spielberg in His Adventure on Earth." *American Premiere,* July 1982. Reprinted in *Steven Spielberg Interviews.* Lester D. Friedman and Brent Notbohm, eds. Conversations with Filmmakers Series. Peter Burnette, general editor. Jackson: University Press of Mississippi, 2000.

Rubin, Susan Goldman. *Steven Spielberg: Crazy for Movies.* New York: Harry N. Abrams, Inc., 2001.

Saathoff, Kenneth G., and Nicole G. White. "*Jaws* Draws." *Harvard Crimson,* April 19, 2006. www.thecrimson.com.

Sanello, Frank. *Spielberg: The Man, The Movies, The Mythology.* Dallas: Taylor, 1996.

Santelmann, Neal. Lifestyle Feature: "Most Expensive Cowboy Boots." *Forbes,* April 4, 2006. www.forbes.com.

Schickel, Richard. "Slam! Bang! A Movie Movie." *Time*. June 15, 1981. Reprinted in *Steven Spielberg Interviews*. Lester D. Friedman and Brent Notbohm, eds. Series: Conversations with Filmmakers. Peter Burnett, general editor. Jackson: University Press of Mississippi, 2000.

Schiff, Stephen. "Seriously Spielberg." *New Yorker*, March 21, 1994. Reprinted in *Oskar Schindler and His List: The Man, the Book, the Film, the Holocaust and Its Survivors*. Thomas Fensch, ed., introduction by Herbert Steinhouse. Forest Dale, VT: Paul S. Eriksson, 1995.

————. "Seriously Spielberg." *New Yorker*, March 21, 1994. Reprinted in *Steven Spielberg Interviews*. Lester D. Friedman and Brent Notbohm, eds. Conversations with Filmmakers Series. Peter Burnett, general editor. Jackson: University Press of Mississippi, 2000.

Schindler's List: Images of the Steven Spielberg Film. Foreword by Steven Spielberg. New York: Newmarket Press, 2004.

Schodolski, Vincent J. "Universal adds a bang to famed tram tour." *Chicago Tribune*, May 28, 2006. www.chicagotribune.com.

Schwinn, Elizabeth, and Ziya Serdar Tumgoren. "The Megagift Plunge." *Chronicle of Philanthropy*, February 20, 2003. www.philanthropy.com.

Science Fiction Museum and Hall of Fame (Seattle). "The Stars Align at the Science Fiction Museum and Hall of Fame: Steven Spielberg, Philip K. Dick, Chesley Bonestell and Ray Harryhausen Represent SRM's First Hall of Fame Class," March 28, 2005. www.sfhomeworld.org.

Scott, A.O. "The Boys of Summer, 30 Years Later." *The New York Times*, July 10, 2005, p. 2.18. www.proquest.umi.com.

Scott, Walter. "Walter Scott's Personality Parade." *Parade*. *Seattle Times*, July 24, 2005. p. 2.

Scott, Walter. "Walter Scott's Personality Parade." *Parade*. *Seattle Times*. September 11, 2005. p. 2.

————. "Walter Scott's Personality Parade." *Parade*. *Seattle Times*, January 1, 2006. p. 2.

Seattle Times. "Beijing Olympics get directors' touch." www.seattletimes. nwsource.com (undated electronic work).

Selective Service System. "Arnold Spielberg Receives Meritorious Service Award." *The Register*, July–August 1999.

Sheffield, Brandon. "EALA's Neil Young on Emotion, IP, and Overtime." Gamasutra Features, May 22, 2006. www.gamasutra.com.

Siegel, Tatiana. "Starry night." *Hollywood Reporter*, March 29, 2005, p. 14(1). www.web2.infotrac.galegroup.com.

Silverman, Stephen M. "Tom Cruise Surprises Steven Spielberg," July 17, 2006. www.people.aol.com.

Simon, John. Review of *Amistad*. *National Review*, December 31, 1997. www. web7.infotrac.galegroup.com.

————. "*Saving Private Ryan.*" *National Review*, August 17, 1998, p. 52(1). www.web7.infotrac.galegroup.com.

Sinclair, Tom. "Christopher Walken: *Catch Me If You Can.*" *Entertainment Weekly*, February 21, 2003, p. 45. www.find.galegroup.com.

Sindt, Nancy Pier, and Hedda T. Schupak. "Spielberg Receives David Yurman Award." *Jewelers Circular Keystone*, January 2000, p. 56. www.find.galegroup.com.

Smith, Sean. "The King of the Worlds; Spielberg talks about movies, terror and wonder, and why the *Oprah* thing bothered him—but only a little." *Newsweek*, June 27, 2005, p. 58. www.web2.infotrac.galegroup.com.

Snow, Michelle. "Spielberg Speaks On Benchley's Death." Bella Online: The Voice of Women. Entertainment News. www.bellaonline.com (undated electronic work).

Sorkin, Andrew Ross. "A Happy Ending for Some, a Comedy of Errors for Others." *The New York Times*, March 12, 2006. www.nytimes.com.

Special Introduction by Steven Spielberg, A. Disc 1. *E.T. the Extra-Terrestrial*, DVD, directed by Steven Spielberg. Two-disc limited collector's edition. Widescreen version. Universal City, CA: Universal Home Video, 2002.

Sporich, Brett. "DVD, VHS fans in hot pursuit of *Catch Me.*" *Hollywood Reporter*, May 15, 2003, p. 15(1). www.find.galegroup.com.

Sragow, Michael. "A Conversation with Steven Spielberg." *Rolling Stone*, July 22, 1982. Reprinted in *Steven Spielberg Interviews*. Lester D. Friedman and Brent Notbohm, eds. Conversations with Filmmakers Series. Peter Burnette, general editor. Jackson: University Press of Mississippi, 2000.

Stax. "Indy 4, JP IV Buzz." IGN Film Force, March 9, 2006. www.filmforce.ign.com.

————. "Ra's Seeing *Red.* Watanabe, Clint team-up." IGN Film Force, March 10, 2006. www.filmforce.ign.com/articles.

————. "Spielberg Beset By Demons?" IGN Film Force, May 15, 2006. www.filmforce.ign.com.

————. "Spielberg Talks *Transformers!*" IGN Film Force, July 20, 2005. www.filmforce.ign.com.

"Steven Spielberg." *American Decades.* Gale Research, 1998. Reproduced in *Biography Resource Center.* Farmington Hills, MI: Thomson Gale, 2005. http://galenet.galegroup.com/servlet/BioRC.

————. Authors and Artists for Young Adults. Vol. 24. Gale Research, 1998. Reproduced in *Biography Resource Center.* Farmington Hills, MI: Thomson Gale, 2005. http://galenet.galegroup.com/servlet/BioRC.

————. *Contemporary Authors Online*, Gale, 2005. Reproduced in *Biography Resource Center.* Farmington Hills, MI: Thomson Gale, 2005. Entry update: September 9, 2004. www.galenet.galegroup.com.

————. *Encyclopedia of World Biography*, 2nd ed. 17 Vols. Gale Research, 1998. Reproduced in *Biography Resource Center*. Farmington Hills, MI: Thomson Gale, 2006. http://galenet.galegroup.com/servlet/BioRC. Accessed July 5, 2006.

Steven Spielberg and the Original *War of the Worlds*. Special Features. *War of the Worlds*, DVD, directed by Steven Spielberg. Two-disc limited edition. Universal City, CA: DreamWorks Home Entertainment, 2005.

Storm, Jonathan. "Spielberg's *West* worth seeing." *Philadelphia Inquirer* (via Knight-Ridder/Tribune News Service), June 9, 2005. www.web2.infotrac. galegroup.

Sunshine, Linda, ed. *E.T. the Extra-Terrestrial. From Concept to Classic*. Introduction by Steven Spielberg. The Illustrated Story of the Film and the Filmmakers Series. New York: Newmarket Press, 2002.

The New York Daily News. "Close Encounters of the Academy Kind," February 27, 2006. www.nydailynews.com.

Thomas, Karen. "Actors Look Back at Moments with Steven Spielberg." Gannett News Service. *The Houston Post*, March 22, 1994. Reprinted in *Oskar Schindler and His List: The Man, the Book, the Film, the Holocaust and Its Survivors*. Thomas Fensch, ed., introduction by Herbert Steinhouse. Forest Dale, VT: Paul S. Eriksson, 1995.

Thompson, Anne. "Hollywood agencies overshadowed by monolith." Yahoo! News, March 24, 2006. www.news.yahoo.com.

————. "Making History: How Steven Spielberg Brought *Schindler's List* to Life." *Entertainment Weekly*, January 21, 1994. Reprinted in *Oskar Schindler and His List: The Man, the Book, the Film, the Holocaust and Its Survivors*. Thomas Fensch, ed., Introduction by Herbert Steinhouse. Forest Dale, VT: Paul S. Eriksson, 1995.

Thompson, David. "Presenting Enamelware." *Film Comment*, March–April 1994. Reprinted in *Oskar Schindler and His List: The Man, the Book, the Film, the Holocaust and Its Survivors*. Thomas Fensch, ed., Introduction by Herbert Steinhouse. Forest Dale, VT: Paul S. Eriksson, 1995.

Toppman, Lawrence. "Nature will take film fest by storm." *Charlotte Observer*, April 2, 2006. www.thestate.com.

Torre, Nestor U. "DiCaprio, Hanks and Spielberg work well together." *Philippine Daily Inquirer*. Asia Africa Intelligence Wire, February 1, 2003. www.web7. infotrac.galegroup.com.

Travers, Peter. Review of *Minority Report*. *Rolling Stone*, July 18, 2002. www. rollingstone.com.

Tuchman, Mitch. "Close Encounters with Steven Spielberg." *Film Comment*, January–February 1978. Reprinted in *Steven Spielberg Interviews*. Lester D. Friedman and Brent Notbohm, eds. Conversations with Filmmakers Series.

Peter Burnette, general editor. Jackson: University Press of Mississippi, 2000.

Turan, Kenneth. "Steven Spielberg." *Smithsonian*, November 2005, pp. 110–111.

———. "Crossroads: Steven Spielberg." *Los Angeles Times*, December 28, 1998. Reprinted in *Steven Spielberg Interviews*. Lester D. Friedman and Brent Notbohm, eds. Conversations with Filmmakers Series. Peter Burnette, general editor. Jackson: University Press of Mississippi, 2000.

TVGuide.com. "Steven Spielberg." www.online.tvguide.com (undated electronic work).

UPI NewsTrack. "Spielberg honored by International Emmys." United Press International, April 25, 2006. www.upi.com.

———. "Spielberg sees virtual actors coming." United Press International, June 19, 2005. www.web2.infotrac.galegroup.com.

———. "Spielberg voted top director." United Press International, June 2, 2005. www.infotrac.galegroup.com.

U.S. Senate. "Tribute to Mr. Arnold Spielberg," April 6, 2001. www.thomas.loc.gov.

USA Today. "Some of Jon Stewart's Oscar Lines." March 5, 2006. www.azcentral. com. Accessed August 25, 2006.

———. "Spielberg's Family Values." June 23, 2005. www.usatoday.com.

Valley, Jean. "*The Empire Strikes Back* and So Does Filmmaker George Lucas with His Sequel to *Star Wars*." *Rolling Stone*, 1980. Reprinted in *George Lucas Interviews*. Sally Kline, ed. Jackson: University of Mississippi, 1999.

Vanneman, Alan. "Steven Spielberg: A Jew in America." *Bright Lights Film Journal* 41 (August 2003). www.brightlightsfilm.com.

Verniere, James. "Holocaust Drama is a Spielberg Triumph." *Boston Herald*, December 15, 1993. Reprinted in *Oskar Schindler and His List: The Man, the Book, the Film, the Holocaust and Its Survivors*. Thomas Fensch, ed., Introduction by Herbert Steinhouse. Forest Dale, VT: Paul S. Eriksson, 1995.

Verrier, Richard. "Exporting thrills." *Baltimore Sun*, April 29, 2006. www. baltimoresun.com.

Wayne, Gary. "Dive!" Seeing Stars: Restaurants owned by the stars. www. seeing-stars.com. Accessed December 4, 2006.

We are not alone. Special Features. *War of the Worlds*, DVD, directed by Steven Spielberg. 2-disc limited edition. Universal City, CA: DreamWorks Home Entertainment, 2005.

WFTV. "Jackie Chan, Bono Among Forbes 'Most Generous Celebrities,'" May 10, 2006. www.wftv.com.

White, Cindy. "*Minority Report*." www.scifi.com (undated electronic work).

Wikipedia. "The Irving G. Thalberg Memorial Award." www.en.wikipedia.org. Accessed May 29, 2006.

————. "Steven Spielberg." www.en.wikipedia.org. Accessed April 18, 2006.

Williams, Rachel. "Novel taken off the shelves after author's confession," April 29, 2006. www.news.scotsman.com.

Wills, Dominic. "Steven Spielberg Biography," December 15, 2005. www.tiscali.co.uk.

WorldScreen.com. "Spielberg to Receive International Emmy Founders Award," April 24, 2006. www.worldscreen.com.

Wuntch, Philip. *The Terminal.* *Dallas Morning News* (via Knight-Ridder/Tribune News Service), June 15, 2004. www.web7.infotrac.galegroup.

Xinhua. "Two world class filmmakers meets [sic] in Beijing." *People's Daily* Online, April 18, 2006. www.english.people.com.cn.

Yahoo! Movies. "Kathleen Kennedy Biography." www.movies.yahoo.com (undated electronic work).

————. "Steven Spielberg Biography." www.movies.yahoo.com (undated electronic work).

Yahoo! News. "Movie stars can't crack top 10 of L.A.'s richest," May 15, 2006. www.news.yahoo.com.

————. "Soros to buy DreamWorks library for 900 million dollars," March 17, 2006. www.news.yahoo.com.

————. *Transformers* Movie Boosts Local Economy," April 30, 2006.

INDEX

About the Author

KATHI JACKSON is the author of *They Called Them Angels: American Military Nurses of World War II* (Westport, CT: Praeger, 2000). She has also written essays for the *Seattle Times*, the *Denver Post*, and *The Herald* of Everett, Washington.